Caring for Yourself

Caring for Your Neurodivergent Child

Diane Reid Lyon
MA, LCMHC, NCC

UNITED WRITERS PRESS
ASHEVILLE, N.C.

ISBN: 978-1-961813-80-9 (trade paper)
ISBN: 978-1-961813-81-6 (eBook)

Published by:

United Writers Press
Asheville, N.C.
www.uwpnew.com

Printed in the U.S.A.

DEDICATION

This book is dedicated to the parents of neurodivergent children everywhere. You have been entrusted with the important job of caring for a very special human being. Despite the challenges you will face along the way, may you stay strong, focus on the positive and hold onto hope. Know you are not alone on this journey. Take care of yourself and you will not just survive, you will thrive!

Contents

ACKNOWLEDGMENTS

I was in a writers group for about a year when I considered giving up on my idea to write a book. I had written maybe 50 pages and was struggling to motivate myself, to believe in myself, to continue on with my writing. Then, out of the blue, I received a call from Ken Garfield, a former journalist with *The Charlotte (N.C.) Observer*. He was calling me about something else.

As we were getting ready to hang up, he mentioned that he now helps people publish books. He asked me if I knew of anyone who wanted to get edited and published. "Ummm... me!" I told him. When Ken agreed to work with me, it was clear in that moment that this was my calling. I was meant to put this book out there into the universe. Thank you, Ken, for believing in me and supporting me through my own grief as it surfaced through the writing process.

I want to give special thanks to the parents who were willing to be interviewed for this book. Their honest, vulnerable sharing helped me to identify themes to focus on in the book. Their voices helped to normalize the experience of raising children with neurodivergence, providing validation to other parents on this journey.

I am grateful also to:

my designer Vally Sharpe and United Writers Press;

my writers group with Anne Bartolucci for supporting me as I started this book;

my past employers, Community Therapeutic Day School, Mecklenburg County Child and Adolescent Services, St. Gabriel Catholic School, and the Fletcher School, as well as to my supervisors and work colleagues, all of whom helped me to grow in my knowledge and expertise, including Alan Shapiro, Daniel Reinstein, Sarah Stutts, Dave Verhaagen, Dawn O'Malley, Paul Shaffer, Kathy Cunningham, Theresa Anderson, Jane Tilley, Bess Forshaw, Jane Poston, Jean Parr, Sharyn Eisdorfer and many others. Many of you also became close friends and supported me on this journey;

my friends, Maria Whitney, Hope Grady, Jen Schere, Karen Fletcher, and Gretchen Deutsch, for lifting me up when life's turbulence kicked me in the butt;

my cousin, Teresa Hendricks, who has been there for me throughout my life;

my brother, Mark Reid, and sister, Carolyn Michalet. I couldn't have gotten through the trying times without you by my side;

my parents, Gloria Kuczminski (deceased), Ignacy Kuczminski (deceased), Roger Reid (deceased) and Maggie Reid, for always encouraging me and equipping me with grit and a growth mindset;

my mother- and father-in-law, Sybil and Richard Lyon, for embracing me as your own and welcoming me and my girls into your family;

our friends, Kristy and Greg Privette, for helping us to rediscover joy by bringing lots of laughter and pickleball into our lives in more recent times, and to Kristy for her input on the book;

Acknowledgments

my therapist, John Burns, for helping me to heal from some of life's traumas and for reminding me to take care of myself. Thank you to the other professionals in our lives for providing assistance along the way;

my colleagues in my peer consultation group for helping me survive through COVID-19 and who continue to offer professional support;

my prayer group for helping me to stay strong in my faith;

my poetry group for providing a creative outlet; *and*

my husband, Dave, for growing with me, for supporting me with this project, and for helping me realize this dream. Thank you for giving me the time and space to write, even when it meant sacrificing our time together. I love and appreciate you.

Most importantly, thank you to our children. I feel privileged to be a part of your lives. You are each unique in your own ways and have such incredible talents. Your perseverance through the drama life has thrown at you is awe-inspiring. It is an honor to witness and be a part of your growth into the amazing humans you are!

Introduction
WHY THIS BOOK?

This book is a self-care guide for parents of neurodivergent children. It is also for those who have primary responsibility for raising and caring for a neurodivergent child, a relative perhaps or non-family member. It is meant to help you — moms, dads and other caregivers — appreciate the importance of taking care of yourselves as you care for your child. This won't just be a pep talk. I won't offer false hope. Instead I will share practical suggestions on how to maintain your health and optimism while on this journey.

There's more...

In the pages that follow, I will focus on how to seek an evaluation for your child when you suspect he may be neurodivergent. I will share information on how to advocate for your child in school. I will refer to other resources intended to help manage behaviors you may face in parenting your kiddo. I will identify and normalize the emotional process parents go through in raising a neurodivergent child. I refer to this as a grief process. I will offer strategies to help you manage feelings of grief. I will discuss and identify signs of burnout and suggest self-care practices to help prevent or recover from burnout. I will help identify when to seek professional help, such as when grief and/or burnout turn into significant anxiety or depression or when there may even be trauma that you have endured. I will also speak to the importance of making meaning out of this journey.

How you manage your own emotions and reactions to your child is key to fostering a positive bond with your child, and in helping your child learn to manage his or her own feelings and behaviors.

My goal is to help you show up as the best version of yourself, on behalf of those who mean the most to you...your children.

As a therapist, I'm not accustomed to sharing a lot about myself, though we therapists do share on occasion as it helps communicate understanding and empathy. Self-disclosure can also deepen the therapeutic relationship with our clients if done correctly, helping create safety and trust and facilitating vulnerable sharing. My purpose in telling you about myself here is to give credence to my professional experience and the contents of this book. I also intend to humanize therapists as we, too, have our own struggles in parenting and can struggle with our own mental health. We, too, are at the whim of what life throws our way.

So I also share on behalf of other therapists who may be reading this book, to help you know that it's OK if you don't have it all together. It's OK, and important, to recognize when you are struggling and to reach out for help as needed. Our struggles don't necessarily impact our professional work so long as we are maintaining good boundaries and taking care of ourselves. In fact, I believe our own struggles can make us better at what we do, as we can bring greater empathy and understanding to our work on behalf of clients and families.

So here's a little bit about me, my background and professional experience. Much of my life has been devoted to children both through my work as well as in raising children of my own. I have worked with children ever since my college days at the University of Rochester in upstate New York. I spent summer breaks working in a day care center and giving swim lessons to children. After college, I worked in a day treatment center for at-risk children for a year. I enjoyed this work so much that I decided to go on to graduate school at Lesley College in Cambridge, MA. There I earned a Master's Degree in Clinical Mental Health Counseling.

My own upbringing, I'm sure, led to my choice to become a counselor. My parents divorced when I was eight years old. I never received counseling as a child to help me through it, though in high school I wrote a research paper exploring the effects of divorce on children, delving into the work of psychologist and researcher Judith Wallerstein. Then during college, I volunteered as a support group facilitator for the Children of Divorce Intervention Program in Rochester, N.Y. I suppose I took my lemons and made lemonade. From my trauma, I looked to help other children who experienced divorce. Perhaps this was also my way of healing my inner child.

I know firsthand the impact mental illness can have on a family and one's home environment. When I was growing up, my stepfather was diagnosed with Bipolar Disorder. He refused medication so he was unmedicated my entire childhood. He most likely had Post-Traumatic Stress Disorder as well, as he was a Holocaust survivor. This was never identified as far as I know. Later, my stepbrother took his life at age 31. This had a significant impact on me and was quite traumatic as well. I took this trauma and turned it around to help others.

First, I did my own grief work. Then I participated in a 26-mile, overnight *Out of the Darkness* walk in Washington D.C., sponsored by the American Foundation for Suicide Prevention (A.F.S.P.). I raised $5,000. I went on to help start a support group in Charlotte, N.C., for survivors of suicide. H.U.G.S (Healing and Understanding of Grief from Suicide) still operates today though I am no longer involved in facilitating this group. I, along with others, brought an A.F.S.P.-sponsored community walk to Charlotte to raise awareness around suicide and to raise money for the A.F.S.P. We also hosted the first National Survivors of Suicide Day in Charlotte. It continues to be held the Saturday before Thanksgiving each year.

This book is another effort on my part to make meaning out of the challenges I have experienced in life as a parent. I will do so through the voices of other parents who experienced similar challenges and agreed to be interviewed for this book.

Isn't it interesting how our life experiences can shape us into who we become and what we decide to do with our lives? I was taught by my parents that there are important lessons to be learned in difficult times. These lessons help us grow. This growth mindset, instilled in me at an early age, helped me develop resilience in the face of some of my most challenging times. Even if we have had challenges or trauma in life, we can learn and grow from these experiences. We can also use these experiences for good if we choose to do so, by helping others. I'll refer to this later as *meaning-making*.

I have been a Licensed Clinical Mental Health Counselor for 30 years. I currently have a private practice in Matthews, N.C., outside Charlotte. Most of my career has focused on counseling children who are considered neurodivergent. That is, they have been identified as having Attention Deficit Disorder, a specific learning disorder, or Autism Spectrum Disorder. Additionally, many of these kids present with anxiety and/or depression. Since behavioral issues often go hand in hand with these conditions, parenting these children leads to greater stress and more challenges for parents.

From my own experience, I share a deep understanding of the struggles parents divulge to me. I see the strain in their weary eyes and hear the desperation in their voices. I recognize the exhaustion they wear like a cloak, weighing heavily on their slumped shoulders. I understand the challenges parents bring to me, such as getting their kids to do basic things like get out of bed to get to school on time or get their homework done and turned in. I understand the envy they feel when they compare their parenting experience to that of others. I empathize with their constant worry over how their children will make it in life. I, too, have had my own struggles as a mom, though I won't be sharing about my own children and parenting out of respect for their privacy.

I will, however, share about my own personal experiences and challenges that led to my writing this book. My first marriage ended in divorce, which left me to function as a single parent for a number of years. I eventually remarried and took on two additional children, doubling my "dirty" laundry (literally and figuratively)! Blending families was not easy, and my husband's and my different parenting styles led to frequent conflict. Our differences created what felt like a war zone in our home at times. This had a negative impact on the entire family. In hindsight, we should have sought professional help sooner.

While managing our mini-Brady Bunch (I sure could have used Alice!), I also oversaw the care of two of my parents—my mom and stepfather—who endured strokes. Luckily, they lived locally so I didn't have to travel far to help with their care, but caring for them while caring for my own family left little to no time for my own self-care.

Then there was loss…

First I lost my mom, who died of a glioblastoma (brain cancer) just 10 days after she was diagnosed. A couple of years later, I lost my dad, followed by my stepfather. I refer to these as my "trying times."

As I was managing all of this in my personal life, I somehow managed to keep my private practice afloat. My work served as a place where I could find relief. Instead of focusing on my own problems, I was able to focus on other people's issues. I did reduce my hours at the time due to the demands of my family life and the stress I was under. And after a caring colleague recommended that I take some time off, I followed her guidance and delved into self-care.

I recognized signs of trauma in myself and sought out a therapist trained in EMDR (Eye Movement Desensitization Reprocessing). EMDR is a treatment to reduce distress around traumatic memories and adverse life events. I landed in John's office. I was not shocked when he diagnosed me with Complex PTSD.

It is important to know that PTSD doesn't only impact those who fight in war. It can strike any of us who are fighting a battle (or more than one) each day of our lives, within our own families and within our own homes, homes meant to be a haven.

Complex PTSD can stem from childhood trauma, ongoing trauma, trauma from multiple events throughout our life or even from severe chronic stress. In my case, I had a history of childhood trauma (my parents' divorce and having a stepfather with mental illness). Additional trauma later in life likely contributed as did the chronic and severe stress and loss I endured through these trying times. I was so busy caring for everyone else that I had neglected caring for myself and it caught up with me!

Through EMDR, the healing process began. Through treatment, I also learned about the importance of self-care. My motto became "If I don't care for myself, no one else will." With EMDR treatment and regular self-care, I gradually began to feel like myself again. I still go to therapy as needed as it is an integral part of my self-care.

A common analogy is used in the mental health field to address the importance of self-care in relation to parenting. The analogy goes something like this: when traveling by airplane we can expect to experience turbulence at times. When we do, there is a chance the oxygen masks could come down. If they do, we are instructed to *put the oxygen mask on ourselves first before we put it on our child*. This is important, as we won't be able to help our child if we don't first help ourselves.

Self-care can be compared to putting on the oxygen mask. Self-care will keep you going when the pressures of parenting exceed your human abilities. You need to see self-care as Priority No. 1. If you don't prioritize self-care, you risk burning out. If you burn out, you will not be able to parent your child as effectively nor enjoy this job that you have been given.

*Parenting these kids can be a rewarding journey—
fun, too—if you take care of yourself.*

This book is not meant to replace professional help though it will help you determine whether you need it. There is no shame in that, EVER. Always remember that if you're in the United States and an emergency arises, call 911 or 988 (the national Suicide & Crisis Lifeline) or go to a local emergency center.

Another air travel analogy. You are about to embark on a journey. Journeys that involve air travel often include layovers at the gate that give you time to recharge. (What else is there to do in a crowded airport?) Consider this book a layover, a place to reevaluate how you are doing with your self-care. Here are the "gates" at which you will be stopping to do just that: Recharge!

- **GATE 1:** I will share (with no names or identifying information to honor their privacy) voices of parents who are on this journey — the challenges and daily victories however small that keep them moving forward. What self-care practices work for them? What advice do they have for you? The best way to learn is from others on the same journey. To those who have allowed me to tell their story, thank you!

- **GATE 2:** What does it mean to be neurodivergent? I will identify the challenges — and benefits — that come with being neurodivergent. I will discuss the importance of recognizing any neurodivergence you might have as a parent and why this is important. I want to address concerns about "labeling" kids. Of course your sons or daughters don't just have "issues," they have gifts to be cherished. It is important to recognize and foster their gifts and talents. Identifying neurodivergence is important as well, as it will help you get your child the help he needs.

- **GATE 3:** I will provide information on how to go about getting your child evaluated and diagnosed, how best to advocate for your child in school and how to request a 504 or IEP (Individualized Education Plan). I will explain what each of these are and when they are needed. I'll also discuss the benefits of getting your child additional help outside of school and when it is time to consider a different school placement.

- **GATE 4:** Grief often comes with parenting a neurodivergent child. I will discuss the importance of recognizing grief (yours, your spouse's, your child's) and finding healthy ways to cope with it. It is critical for you to manage your own feelings and effectively model this for your child.

- **GATE 5:** I will identify common grief-related triggers in parenting neurodivergent children and identify problem-solving strategies to help you come up with solutions for managing these triggers.

- **GATE 6:** I will identify skills to help you self-regulate. This will include coping strategies for managing the stress and feelings of grief in parenting these kiddos. When triggered, how can you respond in a way that is helpful and not harmful?

- **GATE 7:** What are the symptoms of burnout? How can you keep from burning out? What can you do to recover from it? I'll identify self-care practices to incorporate into your daily lives.

- **GATE 8:** Finally, I will discuss the importance of a strong support system and how to build one when family and friends fall short. I will provide other resources — books, websites and more — to help educate and bring inspiration. I will address how to recognize when professional help may be in order, such as when you may have experienced trauma related to parenting your neurodivergent child. I will also discuss the benefits of getting help even when you think you can handle your own problems.

- **POSTSCRIPT:** I will send you off with positive vibes and well wishes, challenging you to make meaning from your parenting journey so you can not just survive but thrive and find joy on this journey

A note to readers: As you continue, you will see that I use the pronoun "he" when referring to a neurodivergent child. Prevalence rates are higher in males than females (girls are typically under-diagnosed). Also, using "he" is less clumsy than using "he or she" throughout the book. Please know that I am referring to both boys and girls.

I hope this book (remember, think of it as a guide) helps you discover life's greatest rewards — love, peace, patience and joy — as you do the hard work of raising neurodivergent children.

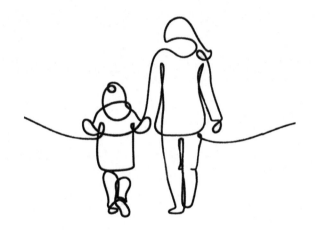

GATE ONE

SHARING YOUR VOICES

The idea for this book was born out of my work with neuro-divergent children. In providing guidance to the parents of these kids, I came to appreciate that they have their own emotions along this parenting journey. In the pages to come, parents give voice to the good days and not-so-good days. They share the victories large and small, and the disappointments that make them more determined to do what's best for their family.

For both the parents who have shared stories here
and the parents who hang on their every word,
I hope you find reassurance in knowing you are
not alone. Together, we go down this road.

I am grateful to the parents who were willing to be interviewed for this book. Many were parents of children I see in my practice. Interviews were done in person or via Zoom. The more informal conversations I regularly have with colleagues and friends also found their way into this book.

Of course, everyone's privacy is honored.

There is little in life more difficult than sharing our deepest emotions, especially when they relate to our children. For parents of children with neurodivergence, these emotions are part of what I have come to recognize as a grief process. I will share more about that—and reflections from parents—in Gate Four, "Grief and So Much More."

Let me give you an overview of what some parents have to say about their parenting journey, starting with the mom who encourages us to take heart. As she says, "Understand that it'll get better."

Exhaustion was a common theme in the interviews. Most parents acknowledged that the challenges they face contribute to emotional and physical exhaustion. Since exhaustion can lead to burnout, I will address burnout later in the book.

Lack of support was another common thread. When I asked one mom if she felt she had adequate support, she said, "Absolutely not! If I didn't seek it out, I wouldn't have had any support." This mom started her own support group.

Many parents were disappointed by the lack of understanding from family and friends. In facing this lack of support, one mom offered a reminder: "Know you are not alone with these struggles/challenges." In other words, there are other parents out there who do "get it."

Later in the book I will address the importance of securing support and offer suggestions about how to find the support you need. I will also share some valuable resources as well as insights into when it's time to seek professional help.

A few parents experienced traumatic events. They dealt with school suspensions due to their child's disability-based behaviors and threats of being arrested for their child's absences. They suffered through their child's medical and/or psychological crises including threats of suicide and suicide attempts. They faced their child's addiction to drugs and alcohol. A few endured their child's aggression toward others and themselves.

One mom expressed fear that her child could become a school shooter. Another feared she would come home and find her child dead by suicide. I will address the trauma arising from these types of experiences in greater detail later.

Despite the struggles, many parents demonstrated great resilience. They all found ways to survive on this arduous journey even if they admitted to not always managing their emotions well.

One father recognized the need for perseverance. Given his frustration about being on a wait list for his child to be evaluated by a psychologist for nearly a year, he advised, "You won't get instant answers (from a psychologist)," he said.

Some parents were in therapy. Some were on medication. Some found other outlets. One Mom identified running as her therapy.

All agreed that self-care (the theme of this book!) is vital even though some acknowledged that it can be difficult to make time for themselves or that they feel guilty when they do so. More on self-care later.

I asked parents, *"What do you wish you knew then that you know now?"* In other words, *"What advice do you have for other parents who are just beginning this journey?"*

Here's what they said:

"I wish I didn't worry as much about the future. Take it one day at a time."

"Try to find more joy and find things you can do together."

"Be preemptive. Contact teachers ahead of time to inform and educate them about your child's needs and what they might see in the classroom. Teach kids to do this for themselves."

"Learn what he learns (i.e. in school courses) so you can be a support."

"Don't let this be the thing the family is centered around."

"Don't bring up struggles all the time. Pick your battles. Celebrate the successes."

"Don't compare your child to others."

"I wish I knew there was more information out there and where to find it."

"Try medication. It is life-changing when it works. Don't give up if one doesn't work. Ultimately it's helping your child. God doesn't make mistakes but does give us resources to help and support us and our child."

"I wish I discovered a Facebook support group sooner. Have a therapist for yourself."

"I would have worked harder to find sitters/respite."

"Prioritize your marriage."

"I wish I knew more about parent/child rights and the law as it pertains to services and what the school should provide. Know your rights and hire an advocate."

"Find peer-to-peer support."

16

"Accept your child for who she is. Don't let others define for you what beauty and humanness is."

"Let your child lead."

"Don't stop believing."

Parents, thank you. Your voices form the heart of this book. Your sharing was powerful, and deeply meaningful to me. You have provided inspiration to all who embrace the wisdom you impart here. By planting seeds of hope for others, I hope this helps you make meaning from your own journey.

GATE TWO

WHAT EXACTLY *IS* NEURODIVERGENCE?

Let me start by explaining neurodiversity. This term was coined by Australian sociologist Judy Singer in the late 1990s. She explains:

> *"Neurodiversity refers to the virtually infinite neuro-cognitive variability within Earth's human population. It points to the fact that every human has a unique nervous system with a unique combination of abilities and needs."**

Singer's point is central to understanding and accepting neurodiversity — those who face the diagnosis, those who help them along the way, and a society that must embrace them both.

Neurodivergent, neuroatypical, even neurospicy are all terms I've heard used to describe the same thing. I will use them interchangeably in this book.

These terms describe the brains of people who process, learn and behave differently as a result of differences in their brain structure and function. Where neuroatypical suggests

---

* http://www.neurodiversityhub.org/what-is-neurodiversity

one's brain is atypical, this is no longer viewed as an *abnormality*. Rather, researchers now recognize the unique strengths and abilities of the neuroatypical brain that are beneficial to the person and to society as a whole.

Neurodivergence may lend to a diagnostic label such as a Specific Learning Disorder/Disability (SLD), Attention Deficit Disorder (ADHD), Autism Spectrum Disorder (ASD), Tourette Syndrome or Dysautonomia.

However, this is not always the case. There can be neurodivergence that doesn't meet diagnostic criteria. Some cultures which are more inclusive and embrace neurodiversity as a gift (different is good!) may not identify and apply diagnostic labels or view neurodivergence through a diagnostic lens at all.

I worked for nearly 10 years in a school with children who were diagnosed with ADHD and/or a learning disability. I continue working with this population in my private practice.

I talk openly with kids and parents about neurodivergence and the more specific labels that identify them as neurodivergent. I explain that in our culture, ADHD and learning disabilities such as *dyslexia* are considered disabilities or disorders.

I unpack the term "disability" for them. "Dis" means "not," I say. "Ability" means "able." I ask them, "Are you not able to learn?"

They invariably offer an emphatic "No!"

I agree with them. "Disability" is not a linguistically accurate term to describe a problem with learning. I reframe this for them, identifying that they have a learning *difference*, not a learning *disability*. I explain that due to a difference in how their mind functions, they learn differently. And because they learn differently they need to be taught differently. I explain that the problem is not with them — it is with our schools and society as a whole, which teaches to the majority, the neurotypical mind.

I also discuss how words like "disorder" and "disability" have a more negative connotation, reflecting the more negative side of differences in brain function. In other words, they pathologize a person. These terms don't reflect the positive traits of these "differences," and there absolutely IS a positive side!

I provide psycho-education to kids and parents alike about ADHD and learning disabilities, reframing any negative connotations they might have. I recognize that kids and parents might feel there is something wrong with them or their child. I talk about these differences as a gift, even as a superpower—a superpower that needs to be honed but nevertheless a superpower.

As I provide a more positive perspective on neurodivergence, I see shifts in body language and facial expressions. Heads hung in shame and defeat suddenly straighten. Eyes that avoided looking at me connect with mine with a renewed sense of hope and possibility. Kids become interested in what I have to say.

I recognize the gifts that come with these labels: curiosity, creativity, spontaneity, passion and compassion, remaining calm in a crisis, resilience, pattern recognition, out-of-the-box problem-solving, drive, a sense of humor, a strong sense of fairness and social justice, and risk-taking. I also mention famous people who are or were neurodivergent—George Washington, Abe Lincoln, John F. Kennedy, Albert Einstein, Steve Jobs and Michael Phelps among many others. These names are often met with wide eyes, as if I've lit a candle of hope within.

I help parents understand that their expectations may need to shift and that traditional parenting approaches may not work. I encourage them to be open to trying different strategies. I suggest that they need to help their child learn good habits and strategies to aid executive function deficits such as problems with attention/focus, time management, planning and prioritizing, initiation of tasks, organization, motivation, flexibility, self-control and perseverance. I explain that discipline means to "educate," not punish. I recognize they may have to help their child learn to manage their emotions and behavioral reactions. I coach them about the importance of modeling for their child by remaining calm in interactions with them. I recognize this will require much patience on their part, plus tons of grace. I also encourage parents to learn about their child's diagnoses if they have been given one.

Information is empowering and will help you better understand your child so you can better advocate for him or her.

As the parents with whom I work learn about their child's diagnosis, they may start to recognize that they, too, may be neurodivergent. Perhaps one or both parents were never identified or diagnosed as such.

Owning your neurodivergence and being open about it with your child is vital to your child learning to accept himself.

I have found that when parents are in denial of their own neurodivergence, they are more likely to project their negative emotions onto their child. This projection may reflect the negative feelings a parent has about him or herself and the struggles they may have had as a child or continue to have as an adult. This projection may also reflect the negative reactions they have received from others throughout their lifetime. In essence, the parent is repeating how others treated him or her. For a mother or father to choose to parent differently, it takes conscious ownership and recognition that "I was like my kid at her age and I don't want her to feel the same way I did about herself" or "I don't want to parent in the same way I was parented." A parent might recognize that they or their spouse struggled in life and worry that their child will struggle similarly. This can get projected onto the child as well, creating anxiety for the child.

Conscious ownership of neurodivergence in the family system and awareness of one's own emotions around this is critical.

I was diagnosed with ADHD at age 50. I suspected I might have it, but getting diagnosed by a medical doctor was affirming. It helped me better understand and accept myself. Instead of thinking of myself as "scatterbrained," I could now say "I sure am easily distracted!" It helped me understand why I had a difficult time being consistent in my parenting and remembering the many things I needed to do to manage my children's lives and schedules as well as my own. It helped me be gentler with myself and give myself grace.

Getting on medication was extremely helpful. I describe it like this: Before medication, my brain was like a black-and-white TV with a fuzzy image and poor antenna lending to stations coming in and out almost constantly. Once on medication, my brain became more like a high-definition color TV with clarity of thought and focus. "This was how most people's minds worked?" I thought to myself. "Wow!" I hadn't realized medication could help so much. Before taking medication, I would come home exhausted after a full day of clients. Once I started medication, I found I had a lot more energy at the end of the day.

Sometimes parents don't want to have their child evaluated because they don't want their kid to be labeled. However, I tell parents that one way or another their kid will get labeled. It is better to have a child identified with ADHD than be labeled as not trying hard enough, lazy, unmotivated, irresponsible, unreliable, flaky, oversensitive, rude, uncaring, selfish, spacey, out of control, stupid, etc.

These are some of the negative labels that will get placed on kids who don't receive a proper diagnosis. Even with a proper diagnosis, your child might still receive some of these negative labels by people who don't understand the diagnosis. The diagnosis is important in that it helps kids qualify for services and medical interventions that may be needed, such as getting a 504 plan or an IEP (Individualized Educational Plan) in school or getting on medication.

If you suspect your child could be neuroatypical, there are options for how to go about getting a proper diagnosis. You can start with your pediatrician. Some pediatricians will diagnose ADHD and Autism Spectrum Disorder. I prefer to refer to a neuropsychologist. This is not the same as a psychologist. A neuropsychologist specializes in diagnosing neurodivergence. This can be an expensive route but one I recommend. A neuropsychologist will spend significantly more time with your child than a pediatrician (often three days of testing) and will do a more thorough assessment of all that may be contributing to your child's symptoms. It is important to let the neuropsychologist know there is neurodivergence in the family or that you suspect your child may be neurodivergent. The more information you provide — what you are noticing, what teachers have reported, what your child has shared — the better.

A proper diagnosis will help you better understand your child. This will help build empathy and understanding, which are the building blocks of patience and grace. For a child, understanding a diagnosis can mitigate low self-esteem. These are the benefits of getting a proper diagnostic label.

Once testing is complete, you will receive a comprehensive report from the neuropsychologist that will serve as a map of your child's mind. It will identify your child's IQ. This is helpful as most people with neurodivergence have average to above-average intelligence. This helps parents and kids recognize that intelligence is not the issue. Indeed, you have a smart kid! Strengths and weaknesses as far as learning will also be identified. Recommendations will be given regarding how your child learns best. Strategies will be suggested that may help support deficits. Your child will receive a diagnosis which, as I mentioned, may prove helpful if you choose to seek school interventions such as an IEP or 504 plan (more on that later).

If money is an issue, you can request testing by your public school, which will be free. Be mindful that the psychologist works for the school, so there is potential for bias. What I mean by this is that their recommendations may be limited to what the school can and is willing to provide.

It may also be prudent to see a neurologist to confirm any diagnosis received, and to rule out any other neurological conditions that could be contributing to your child's symptoms. I recall a student at the school where I worked who was struggling to retain information. Although previously diagnosed with a learning disability, his parents took him to a neurologist. Come to find out he was having absence seizures, which were not previously identified. Absence seizures are a form of petit mal seizures that are not obvious and may just involve staring off into space. Once these seizures were identified and the child put on the proper seizure medication, his ability to learn and retain information improved.

Once you have a diagnosis, it is important to get your child the help and support he or she needs. Don't overfocus on your child's deficits, though. Don't run yourself ragged taking your child to all kinds of specialists. This will only lead to burnout for you and your child. It is important to prioritize your child's needs and to focus on one or two areas at a time.

Don't forget, you have an incredible child with all kinds of strengths and talents. Build on these strengths and talents. These may lead your child to a fulfilling career one day, or at least to hobbies and activities that your child can enjoy. Your child's strengths and talents will also help build self-esteem and lead them to be happy.

If your child is happy, you will be, too!

GATE THREE

SUPPORTING YOUR CHILD IN SCHOOL AND BEYOND

Having a neurodivergent child affords you the responsibility—and privilege—of being their advocate. This includes helping them get the most out of their education. Consider this chapter a primer on navigating the tricky journey through school.

Obtaining An IEP Or 504 Plan

With a proper diagnosis, children in public school by law may qualify for an Individual Education Plan (IEP) under the Individuals with Disabilities Act (IDEA) or a 504 plan under Section 504 of the Rehabilitation Act of 1973.

An IEP outlines goals and objectives for specialized instruction to help address areas of delay or deficit. If your child has an IEP, he will typically leave the classroom and receive small group or individual instruction from a special education teacher, speech/language therapist or occupational therapist.

A 504 plan on the other hand provides accommodations in the classroom. These accommodations are provided by the classroom teacher. They could include things like preferential seating (sitting in the front of the class or near the teacher) to help minimize distractions, extended time on tests or projects, a separate setting for taking tests or a reduced workload. There are other accommodations that could also be added to a 504 plan if it is determined to be needed and if approved by the school.

To initiate testing by the school or see if your child qualifies for an IEP or 504 plan, you need to reach out to your school administrator or school counselor. I recommend putting your request for a meeting in writing. Sending an email to the IEP or 504 coordinator directly is the way to go. This way you will have documentation of your request. All communications and requests should be in writing or via email so there is a paper trail. The school has 90 days to meet and discuss your child from the date your request is sent.

Ahead of this meeting, provide documentation to the school confirming your child's diagnosis. They will need to receive a copy of the neuropsychological evaluation or a letter from your child's pediatrician with the diagnosis listed. This will help them to be better prepared for the meeting.

If you don't yet have a diagnosis and want the school to evaluate your child, let them know this as well. Be prepared to bring any documentation you have in support of this request. It could include email exchanges between you and your child's teacher, copies of interim reports and report cards. Make a list of what you are noticing at home including how your child handles homework, how long it takes him to complete homework and behaviors you notice around homework. Share any complaints your child has about school or difficulties he encounters in the classroom or in getting up to go to school.

Note your child's behavior when he comes home from school. Some students mask their emotions during school then melt down once they are home, where they feel safe to do so.

It may be helpful to hire an advocate to help you advocate for your child to be evaluated or to receive a 504 plan or IEP. Sometimes schools resist providing support to children who need it, as the child may not be failing. Giving a child a 504 plan or an IEP means more work for them. Schools may push for students to get a 504 plan rather than an IEP as it is an easy and quick route to attempt to help your child. A 504 plan gives a child accommodations in the classroom, but it does not address different learning needs. Given the lack of special education teachers, schools more than ever prefer to give 504 plans.

Consider hiring an advocate. Advocates have often worked in schools as either a special education teacher, school psychologist or school counselor. They are informed about parents' and students' rights and disability laws. They often know the language that needs to be used to get past the resistance of school administrators so you can obtain needed services for your child. There are also attorneys with expertise in special needs cases who may be helpful if you feel you or your child's rights or disability laws are being violated.

In this case, you can also choose to seek an informal resolution by speaking to your school principal, special education administrator or 504 administrator. A complaint can be filed with the local board of education through the district superintendent or a formal complaint can be made with the IDEA through the state board of education office. You may also file for a "due process hearing." This is similar to a hearing in civil court. If you go this route, the burden of proof is on you as a parent to prove you or your child's rights (or laws) have been violated. You will likely want to hire a lawyer to represent you, though it is not required.

Your child should be re-evaluated every three to five years or at every academic level — elementary school, middle school and high school. This will help you track his progress and keep goals and accommodations current with his developing needs. These evaluations should be shared with the school for the purposes of updating IEPs and 504 plans.

Additional Support

Once your child receives an IEP or 504 plan be sure to keep an open line of communication with your child to make sure he is receiving services or accommodations. You should document when your child reports that he has not received services or accommodations as outlined in his IEP or 504 plan. Be sure to take any concerns about your child failing to receive services to the school administrator. Without documentation, they will not have the proof needed to monitor and ensure service delivery.

Your child may benefit from getting a tutor to support his learning. Often teachers provide extra support before, during or after school for students who need it. Your child shouldn't have to miss recess or PE to get extra support. He needs these breaks and opportunities to get up and move. If your child doesn't have a good relationship with his teacher or if he is concerned about how peers will view this and treat him, you may want to consider hiring a tutor. If your child is in middle or high school, you may need to hire more than one tutor, for instance, one for math and one for language arts. You can try to provide academic support to your child. This may go well. If so, more power to you! Sometimes, though, children resist help from their parents. This may lend itself to conflict in the parent-child relationship. I find this to be especially true when kids get into middle or high school. Their need for support conflicts with their age-appropriate developmental goal, which is to become more independent and not need their parents (as much). Hiring a tutor can help eliminate any conflict in the parent-child relationship.

When To Consider A School Change

If your child is in public school and you don't feel he is making progress or getting the support needed to be successful despite your best efforts to advocate for him, you might want to consider changing schools. Is the school environment more punitive and negative than supportive and helpful? It may be time to consider a school change. Or, if you are facing morning battles regularly around getting your child to school, I highly recommend reading the article: "Why School Stress is Devastating for Our Children" by Jerome Schultz, Ph.D. (www. additude.mag). He has also written a book, though I haven't read it yet — *Nowhere To Hide: Why Kids with ADHD and LD Hate School and What We Can Do About It.*

There are public charter schools that may be more accommodating in meeting your child's needs. Private schools might also better serve your child. There may be grants you can apply for to help pay for private school tuition. Some private schools offer financial aid or scholarships. I've even known a parent who got their health insurance to cover the cost of a specialized school for her child with autism. In some cases, you might be able to get the public school system to pay for a private school. By law, if the public school system cannot serve your child's needs, they are required to pay for an alternative school placement. You will need plenty of documentation demonstrating their inability or refusal to serve your child. Getting the school system to pay for private school may be a battle and likely will involve hiring an attorney and/or going to court.

Teach Your Child To Self-Advocate

Once a child reaches middle school (if not before), he should participate in the 504 plan or IEP meeting. If you suspect the meeting will be contentious perhaps only have your child participate at the beginning to voice how school is going and what support he needs in the classroom to ensure success. Don't force this. But offer the opportunity to your child. I suggest you also have your child reach out to his teacher via email before school starts to introduce himself. He should share about his individual interests and strengths and weaknesses when it comes to learning and what helps him achieve success in the classroom. Have your child attach a copy of his 504 plan or IEP to the email so the teacher has a copy. That way the teacher cannot say he or she didn't know your child had a 504 plan or IEP or didn't receive a copy of it.

No matter where they are in school, empower your child to advocate for himself.

Sometimes substitute teachers are not aware when children have 504 plans or IEPs. I recommend having your child keep a copy of the 504 plan or IEP in a binder so he can present this to the teacher in support of his learning needs.

Encourage your child to speak up when he doesn't understand something in the classroom. Especially in middle school and high school, encourage him to communicate with teachers himself. You can provide guidance on how to go about this. You might help him draft an email to the teacher and provide this level of support until your child is ready to do this independently. I can't say enough about how important it is that you teach your child to self-advocate. This will help prepare him to do so for himself when you aren't there to do it for him, such as when he goes to college or lands a job.

Your child may get to an age where he is embarrassed to be "different" and may not want to use his accommodations. Help your child understand that his accommodations are meant to help ensure his success, which is more important than how he is perceived by his peers (though he may not see it this way). Help him learn how to respond to any questions or flak he receives from his peers. Help your child know that everyone has different needs when it comes to learning and that how he learns best may not be how others learn best. If accommodations are helpful and ensure success, that's a good thing.

When You Need To Advocate

I encourage you to fight hard if your child's school is trying to take away your child's 504 plan or IEP unless you believe your child no longer needs it and can function well without it. It is possible your child has met IEP goals and is on grade level and no longer needs it. However, if a school wants to do away with it at a transitional year such as fifth grade, advocate to keep it in place until you can see how your child adjusts to middle school and the increased workload. If the school claims your child isn't asking for his accommodations outlined in the 504 plan, inform the school that it is their responsibility to provide accommodations, not your child's responsibility to have to ask for them.

Preparing For College

If your child requires accommodations in the classroom, he will likely need them for the ACT or SAT. The College Board requires documentation that your child needs these accommodations in school. Encourage your child to use his accommodations as he will risk losing them if he doesn't. I've seen kids lose their 504 plans when refusing accommodations, then not be able to get accommodations for the ACT or SAT.

Before college, your child will need a fairly current (within two years) evaluation. Your child's success in college will largely be determined by his willingness to accept and use his accommodations in college and to advocate for his needs. If your child is on medication, it's critical that he continue to take it as prescribed. I often recommend that neurodivergent kids start out at community college or consider doing a fifth year of college. This way they can take a lighter load each semester, which will help ensure their success.

Other Options Besides College

Not all neurodivergent kids go on to college or go to college right away. Some may take a gap year or choose to work for a while. Encouraging college is fine, though forcing it is not recommended. I have known students whose parents pushed college and ended up losing a lot of money as a result of their child dropping or flunking out. Your child needs to be ready for this responsibility. Not all kids are ready when their peers are. It is never too late to go to college. This is a good message to send your child. Let him know he can always go to college later. I had an aunt who went back and earned her Bachelor's Degree when she was in her 60s. It is great to share examples of other people who do this. I recently read about Minnie Payne, who graduated with her Master's Degree from the University of North Texas at age 90, *seven decades after she completed high school.* Emphasize to your child that they have their own timeline, one that is unique to them.

Recognize the benefits and learning your child will gain from other experiences, such as having a job, traveling or having a gap-year experience. Support your child's choices.

Know this. How your son or daughter shows up to school as a young child does not predict future success in a job. I have known children who got to work on time and managed their work responsibilities, yet in school they struggled to do the same. When I asked one child what the difference was, he said, "It's simple really. I hate school and I love my job. And I make money!"

Jobs involve more hands-on learning, which neurodivergent children tend to enjoy and be good at. Getting paid is also its own reward.

There are plenty of examples of people with neurodivergence who did not go to college and worked their way up in a company. If your child is adamant about not going to college, share some of these positive examples. Let him know that if he works hard and demonstrates an interest in learning and growing in a company, there may be opportunities for advancement.

Another option your child might consider is going to trade school or into the military.

Hiring a career counselor or meeting with a career counselor at the community college might help your child find a direction he is interested in. There are also online assessments your child can take to identify possible career paths.

Whatever direction your child takes in life, always show up to support him rather than criticize or judge him for his choices. With your support, your child will grow into his full potential. By instilling your belief in him, your child can come to believe in himself as well!

GATE FOUR

GRIEF AND SO MUCH MORE

I will refer to the emotional process of coming to terms with neurodivergence in one's self, one's child or family system as a grief process.

If you are familiar with the Peanuts comic strip, Lucy was infamous for exclaiming, "Good grief, Charlie Brown!" What did she mean by this? It was her way of expressing her exasperation with the round-faced, woebegone character. She would get so frustrated with him, just as you might get frustrated with your ankle-biter at home. Lucy expressed her grief. That is a good thing, though you might want to be a little kinder than Lucy was to Charlie Brown. Awareness of your grief allows you to be more in control of your emotions so you can consciously choose how to manage your feelings.

Grief is typically associated with a death. Who would ever expect to feel grief as a parent of a living, breathing little being? Surprise! Grief can be experienced anytime there is a loss or change of any kind — leaving a job (even if it's your choice) or moving, for example. That last one may involve loss as you leave behind a home you've grown familiar with as well as friends, a neighborhood or community.

A child may feel grief in transitioning to a new school as he misses his old one. Grief may surface in starting a new school year as the freedom and joys of summer are missed. A young adult might experience grief in leaving home for the first time to go off to college as he says goodbye to his childhood, family and pets. A young adult may experience grief in coming to terms with not having had the ideal parents or childhood. Losing a pet can lend itself to grief. Getting married can cause cold feet for some, which can be an expression of grief — fear of losing the freedoms that come with being single.

Grief and loss are a part of life.

When you have a child who is atypical and doesn't measure up to the "norm," there is grief, as there is a loss of hopes, dreams and expectations. Grief may be experienced when your child doesn't reach the typical developmental milestones around the time of his peers or when a younger sibling surpasses an older sibling in some ability. You might compare your child to others. When you see your child isn't keeping up in some way, you worry and fret. This is grief. You can grieve for yourself and have grief for your child as well.

At the same time, your child may have his own grief process. As he looks around and notices he is different than his peers, isn't measuring up, isn't meeting expectations of teachers, parents and perhaps others, he grieves. He wonders, "What is wrong with me? Why am I not like my peers? Why can't I do the things my teachers or parents expect of me?"

Family members, though grieving the same loss, may grieve differently. Some may internalize their grief. They hold it in and don't express it. This can lead to anxiety, depression or explosive outbursts. Others may externalize their grief and act it out in meltdowns, more regular angry outbursts, passive-aggressive behavior or obstinance and rebellion. A healthier way of coping with grief is to acknowledge it, talk about it or embrace some other creative outlet to express it. We will explore other ways of managing feelings related to grief later on.

Given that each person's grief process is unique to them, it is important to respect each other's way of grieving. Everyone is different and requires different things when experiencing grief. A wife might want time alone while her husband seeks comfort or vice versa. Navigating these differences can be tricky but not impossible. All it takes is a little communication. With awareness of your grief, you will become better able to identify what you need so that you can better communicate and advocate for yourself. As a couple, you may need to find a way to negotiate your needs when they are in opposition. There is no right or wrong way to grieve, unless it impacts you or others negatively.

STAGES OF GRIEF

It helps to be familiar with the stages of grief identified by Elisabeth Kubler-Ross, MD:

1) Denial
2) Anger
3) Bargaining
4) Depression
5) Acceptance

While these stages were identified in her research on grief as it relates to death and dying, they can be experienced with any type of loss. One can move through these stages of grief in any order or bounce back and forth between them. It is not always a neat and orderly progression. It is even possible to *not* experience all of these stages. In the case of a death, these stages suggest you will eventually reach a place of acceptance. Life goes on, perhaps in a new or different way. But it goes on and your grief resolves.

Instead of thinking of these as "stages," I prefer to think of them as phases or passages. I like this language better. To me, "stages" sound measured and progressive. It suggests that you finish one stage and move to the next. Phases or passages seems to suggest a more fluid process, which is more like how grief is typically experienced. One phase may flow into another, then back again. I will use this language moving forward.

Some grief can be more complicated, such as when there is a loss that is sudden, unexpected or tragic in some way, such as when a child dies or there is a death by suicide. Loss related to divorce or loss associated with having a child who has a chronic medical illness, deformity, disability or is neuroatypical in some way can also involve more complex grief. There may be additional phases of grief one might experience in these cases, and the grief process may be prolonged.

The following phases of grief that I have identified for the purposes of this book are not research-based but rather are drawn from my own experiences as a parent and therapist, and from interviews I conducted with parents of neurodivergent children.

In interviewing parents about the grief process, one mom said it best. "The struggle is real!"

PHASES OF GRIEF WHEN PARENTING NEURODIVERGENT CHILDREN

Shock Or Relief

This phase of grief might come when you first notice or learn your child is struggling, is different in some way or is not developing according to the "norm." Perhaps a teacher expresses concern that your child is having challenges learning to read or behavior problems in the classroom. Shock can come when you have your child evaluated and receive an official diagnosis. You might find yourself thinking or saying, "My child has what?" "How can that be?" "How did this happen?"

Perhaps if you suspect something is not quite right with your child, you might feel relief to discover what it is. Sometimes knowing something is wrong but not knowing what it is can produce anxiety. Getting answers, such as receiving an official diagnosis, can provide relief. A diagnosis may give you something to understand and work with.

One family I interviewed shared that their child was diagnosed with Familial Dysautonomia (FD) as an infant. This is a rare, inherited genetic disorder that can impact the regulation of nervous system functions such as breathing, salivating, swallowing, blood pressure and body temperature. These parents were told at the time that their child's life expectancy was five years old at best. As you can imagine, receiving news like this would come as quite a shock. Thankfully, their child is alive and well today, many years later.

One mother shared that after she received her son's diagnosis, she laid down on the couch and cried as she didn't yet know what this meant for him.

By contrast, one father identified relief in getting a diagnosis. He recognized that it would help his son get what he needs.

Similarly another mom said she felt relief because knowing the diagnosis allowed them to move forward.

One mom had a sister with ADHD. She felt that her experience growing up with her sister helped because she knew her sister turned out okay. Because of that, the mom had a "Let's take care of it!" attitude.

Another mother described feeling relief in getting a diagnosis because it explained some of her daughter's quirks. She also felt that the diagnosis relieved her from feeling that it was her fault in some way.

Denial

Denial is your brain's way of protecting you from a reality that is difficult to face. You may not want to believe your child has any problems. Or you may need time to process a new diagnosis. You may even reject or resist it at first. There are times you might even forget your child is different. You might find yourself thinking or saying something like, "There's nothing wrong with my child." "I was the same way." "He'll outgrow it." "I don't want my kid labeled." "ADHD is just an excuse for bad behavior."

One parent told me, "I didn't want to accept that my daughter was handicapped."

Another parent said she'd sometimes forget her child had a particular issue related to her diagnosis. She recognized that when her child was doing well, the issue wasn't in the forefront of her mind.

One mom mentioned, "His dad didn't grasp needing to deal with him differently."

Another father admitted he would sometimes forget his child had ADHD. He would get frustrated with his child when he didn't follow through with expectations. The father admitted his expectations were sometimes not realistic.

Bargaining

In this phase, you might ask "Why?" "Why my child?" "Why does life have to be so difficult for my child?" You might convince yourself everything will be OK if only...You might find yourself thinking or saying something like, "If I just spend more time with him, he'll be OK." "I'll give him a dollar for every A he gets, that'll work." "If I get him a tutor, he'll be fine." "If I pray harder, God will take care of this."

Bargaining may propel you into trying to "fix" your child.

A mom admitted that when she was in this phase, she asked herself "Why us?" and expressed wanting a "do-over."

Fear/Worry

Fear may come from seeing your child struggle or not knowing how to help him. You might feel fear when you project into the future your worries and concerns for your child. You might find

43

yourself thinking or feeling, "Will he ever learn to read?" "How will he ever graduate?" "How will he manage college?" "How will he hold a job?" "What will happen to him if I die?"

One mom feared getting called by her son's school, so in her phone she labeled his school "Deep Breath." She also feared her son would struggle in after-school activities and that she'd get a call from his coaches.

Another mom expressed worry about how her child's ADHD would impact his learning and performance in school. She identified worry related to whether she was doing enough to help him.

One mom shared about her ADHD/autistic son's aggression and said she was afraid of his "getting in the system" or harming others.

For the family whose child has Familial dysautonomia (FD), their fear centered around life-threatening medical crises. Fear also arose for them when they considered having another child. Would they have another child with FD?

Many of the parents I interviewed expressed fear for their child's future and how they will manage in college and in life.

Fear and even trauma can become a constant companion for parents who experience a child running away or whose child struggles with self-harm, suicidal ideation, suicide attempts, threats of harm to others or aggression toward others.

One dad recognized that parenting neurodivergent kids can lend to being in fight-or-flight mode. "It is survival day to day."

Frustration/Anger/Resentment

You might feel frustrated, angry or resentful. These emotions can lead to blaming yourself or your spouse for your

44

child's differences. You might feel angry with God or even your child. You might find yourself thinking or saying, "This is my husband's fault. He struggled in school, too." Or "Maybe my having an epidural caused this." You might blame your child along the way. "She isn't trying hard enough."

One parent identified feeling angry when things she would do to help her child weren't working.

Another mom identified feeling frustrated when her son "couldn't get it together sometimes."

A dad admitted getting angry in response to his child's behavioral outbursts and disrespect.

Similarly, another mom expressed frustration over her child not being able to do basic self-help or life skills.

One mom whose adult child was still at home identified frustration related to knowing her child would be with them longer and that their work was not ending anytime soon. They realized that parenting was going to require more effort.

Several parents mentioned feeling anger toward their child's school or teachers. They were angry that their child was not getting the needed support to be successful and to feel positive about learning and going to school.

Disappointment/Mourning/Depression

You might feel disappointed that this parenting journey is so difficult. You can experience mourning/depression when you allow yourself to feel sadness associated with grief. You might feel a sense of hopelessness or helplessness, which can go hand in hand with depression. You might find yourself thinking or saying, "I've tried everything. I don't know what more to do." "Things are never going to get better." "She'll never succeed."

One mom I interviewed recognized feeling helpless when seeing her child struggle and not being able to do anything to help. She described it as "gut-wrenching."

Another mom said, "No matter how hard we try, he's still struggling."

One mom identified feeling sad over things her child was missing out on such as the prom and school trips.

Another mom admitted disappointment—her son wasn't a star scholar or couldn't manage being on a sports team.

One mom said, "This is lifelong for her. It's devastating."

Another recognized that comparing her child to peers evoked sadness. She identified exhaustion as leading to depression.

Embarrassment/Shame

You might be embarrassed by your child's behavior in public, by messages or comments you receive from his teacher or calls from the principal. You might be embarrassed that your child is often late to school or refuses to go to school. You might feel embarrassed by meltdowns in public or your child's behavior at birthday parties or other social events. If you feel judged or blamed, you might feel embarrassed. If you internalize it, as if your child's behavior reflects on you or your parenting, you may also experience shame.

One parent felt judgment from others and questioned whether it was real or perceived. She took this on as if "it was my fault." She acknowledged feeling "mortified."

Another mom identified being embarrassed in public when her daughter acted up, recognizing that others aren't likely to understand. She also felt judged or blamed for her daughter's behavior.

One mom felt that her parenting was called into question by her child's school, which contributed to stress and embarrassment. She felt she was "under the microscope."

Guilt

You may feel guilty for something you've done or not done, feeling that it's not enough or too much. You may feel guilty for how you've handled situations or expressed your grief. You may feel guilty when you feel responsible in some way for causing your child's problems or when you are not able to "fix" them. You may find yourself thinking or saying, "It's all my fault." "If only I had..." "I shouldn't have..."

One mom felt guilty when being away from her child so that she (mom) could do something for herself. The mom's guilt came from shifting out of her typical caretaker role to focus on self-care. This is not uncommon for caretaker moms who are first learning self-care.

Another mom identified feeling guilty when her child was overmedicated and it suppressed his positive personality traits.

Several parents acknowledged guilt and even shame related to their reaction at times to their child's behavior.

Envy

You may feel envy when comparing your child or your parenting journey to that of others. You may be jealous of other parents who appear to have easier children, whose children are able to accomplish more, whose children don't have the challenges yours do. You may find yourself thinking or saying, "I wish my child could make the Honor Society just once." "I wish I could switch lives with those parents for just one day." "I wish my child was going to college."

One parent expressed it this way: "I feel envy when I see how easy other parents have it. They didn't get a broken kid. Their kids get to do things my child can't and won't." These kids aren't broken but it might feel that way sometimes.

Isolation/Loneliness

You can feel isolated and lonely as friends or family may not want to be around your child or family due to your child's behaviors. You may not feel you can leave your child with a sitter. You may isolate yourself from others for fear of judgment or rejection. You may find yourself thinking or saying, "No one understands." "I don't have anyone to turn to who gets it." "No one wants to play with my son or have him over to their home."

The mom whose child has FD spoke of going through several respite workers. She identified the isolation that stems from not having others who can care for her child so she can go out with friends.

Another mom felt that her friends didn't understand her situation. Isolation came from avoiding social situations because they could be overstimulating for her child. She also admitted shielding her child from rejection. She found it helpful to connect with other parents who had similar challenges, though.

Another mom acknowledged feeling judged and excluded socially.

Yet another mom admitted avoiding social situations as she didn't know how her child would react with her sensory issues.

But it isn't always that way...

One mom didn't feel that she struggled with isolation or loneliness. She spoke of having the support of a family member who was in the mental health field, and friends who had their own struggles. She recognized that it was helpful to connect with others who had similar struggles.

Self-Doubt

It is natural to have doubts about parenting a neurodivergent child. You are not likely coming into parenting knowing what these kids need or how best to meet their needs. It is natural to question yourself and your parenting.

One parent expressed not ever knowing what was going to help or hurt. She acknowledged questioning whether she was getting it right regarding selecting professionals.

Another mom identified "decision fatigue." She admitted to constantly questioning her decisions.

Another mom questioned what she did wrong or what she could have done differently.

Yet another mom wonders whether she is imagining things or making a bigger deal than it is.

One neurodivergent mom who seemed to embrace her neurodivergent children better than some other parents I interviewed asked, "What if I'm wrong, then what?" She recognized "the variability in being human (and in experiencing these kids) lends to questions, confusion and self-doubt."

Stress/Exhaustion/Feeling Overwhelmed

Let's face it. Parenting neurodivergent children is stressful. You can experience stress from the demands of parenting in general. But the demands are far greater when you have a neurodivergent child. You are not alone if you feel overwhelmed and exhausted from the amount of time, attention and energy required to parent your neurodivergent child. These children have many more needs and are more dependent on parents to help them, and for a longer period of time than neurotypical children.

You can run yourself ragged trying to manage your child's needs if you aren't careful. You can burn out.

Dads often feel more of the stress from the financial responsibility of caring for their families and providing for the needs of a neurodivergent child. Sometimes moms feel this, too, if they are a single mom or the main breadwinner. The reality is that these kids come with a heftier price tag. At a recent workshop I attended on ADHD, I learned that the cost to raise an ADHD child is five times that of a neurotypical child. I would guess a child with autism comes with an even higher price tag.

The family of the child with FD spoke of being exhausted from multiple trips to the hospital and from having to sleep on the floor of their daughter's room when she was sick because it was "always life-threatening." One of her parents commented, "I don't even know if we knew how exhausted we were. We were just doing what we had to do."

Another parent spoke of feeling exhausted "across the board" because she was always thinking and coming up with something to help her child.

One mom recognized that her sense of being overwhelmed came from expectations of all that she felt they needed to do and get done to help their child.

Another mom identified mental exhaustion from "keeping the ship moving forward." She recognized that she was the one providing what her child needed. She mentioned that she didn't work because she felt that if she did it would all fall apart.

One mom shared, "I'm emotionally drained every day. I spend a lot more energy on things with her. Daily tasks are 20 to 50 times harder for her than they should be."

Acceptance

If you allow for the flow of grief, let yourself feel the various emotions and manage the turbulence, you will eventually get to your final destination. You will come to accept your child for who he is with all his struggles. You understand his needs and do your best to meet them. You recognize his talents, passions, and positive personality traits and foster them.

You might find yourself thinking or saying, "I love my child the way he is." "I wouldn't trade him for another." "He has his challenges but also great gifts." "I know he'll find his way although his path may look different from others and it may take him longer to get there."

The parents of the child with FD recognized that they reached this stage as their child got older and became an adult. They recognized that "She is fun to be around and is more of a friend and not as much of a burden." Her mom admits she once wished she had a "normal" child but later said, "I wouldn't trade her now! She's a wonderful person to be with and share life with."

Another parent commented, "She's a great kid to be with and I never wished her to be anyone but herself."

One parent recognized that time helped her get to a place of acceptance. She said, "It's a gradual process and important to recognize that you can't fix this."

Another mom felt she arrived at acceptance when her son was in middle school. But she recognized that she experienced less positive emotions when he got to high school — when things escalated for her son and his differences became more noticeable.

One parent felt she was able to get to acceptance by recognizing her child's growth and progress and by others recognizing how awesome he is. Seeing him happy helped. So did focusing on his interests and strengths.

One mom identified her daughter as "crazy creative, witty and sees the world in her own special way."

Another mom recognized that learning about her son's diagnosis helped her get to acceptance, as did praying and recognizing that "God made him the way he is." She shared: "He's amazing, so smart, he blows us away with his knowledge and his piano-playing."

One mom expressed gratitude that her children are different.

Another said she felt blessed to have the kids she has.

THE PROLONGED GRIEF JOURNEY

It is important to know that as a parent of a neurodivergent child, you are on a prolonged grief journey. You might find yourself experiencing grief at different stages of your child's development as well as your own development. Grief may be experienced throughout your lifetime together or at least until your child is capable of surviving on his own.

Following are some examples of how this prolonged grief may affect your reactions as your child progresses from elementary school through high school and beyond.

In Elementary School

The teacher informs you that your child is struggling with learning or sends home frequent reports of bad behavior. (Shock/frustration/guilt/embarrassment)

You assume the problem your child is having will work itself out in due time. (Denial)

You wonder if something could be wrong. (Worry)

Your child is not able to meet your expectations at home, melts down over homework and struggles to follow directions. (Fear, frustration/anger)

Your child is diagnosed with ADHD. You jump into high gear and attempt to "fix" your child, filling the schedule with after-school appointments with multiple therapists and tutors. You might try all the latest treatments even if they aren't supported by research. (Bargaining)

Conflict erupts between you and your husband. He doesn't think your child needs professionals involved in your lives and sees the money going out in droves. (Frustration/anger/stress)

You blame each other for who passed this on to your child. (Anger/guilt/shame)

You might forget your child is neurodivergent and hold him to more age-appropriate expectations vs. what he is capable of. (Denial, frustration/anger)

You feel alone. All of your time and energy are focused on helping your child. You have stopped doing things with friends. (Isolation/loneliness)

Friends and family members have distanced themselves from you due to your child's behaviors. They blame your child's problems on your parenting. (Anger, isolation/loneliness, guilt, embarrassment/shame, self-doubt)

In Middle School

Without the structure and support provided in elementary school, your child struggles to be independent, organized and responsible. His grades drop due to missing work. He doesn't yet possess the skills to be independent and resists your efforts to help. Conflict ensues. (Fear, frustration/anger)

Your child starts to stand out more from his peers socially. He experiences bullying and rejection. (Fear, sadness, anger)

Your child starts discovering his unique skills and abilities and you recognize that he is unique in his own way. (Acceptance)

In High School

You are exhausted from frantically trying to fix your child and from the many battles that have ensued through the years with your husband, the school and your child over what is needed. (Depression/stress/exhaustion)

You see your child falling behind and giving up. Despite all your efforts, your child still struggles. (Fear, frustration/anger, depression, self-doubt)

You are concerned about how he will survive in the world on his own and whether he can go to college or hold a job to support himself. (Fear)

Other parents are gloating about the honors, rewards, trophies and college acceptances their children are receiving. You wish it was your child. (Envy)

Your child isn't going to college. He will likely remain at home longer, depending on you financially and emotionally until he can stand on his own two feet. You feel like you failed as a parent. (Fear, frustration/anger, depression, embarrassment/shame, self-doubt)

Your child lands a job and shows up in a different way than he did for school. He works hard and is responsible. You realize he has strengths and talents to offer the world and will be okay even if his path doesn't look like you imagined it for him and is different from other kids' paths. (Acceptance)

RECOGNIZING YOUR GRIEF

Learning to identify where you are in this grief process is important. Doing so will help you to be more in control of your emotions. By recognizing the phase of grief you are in, you can talk about your feelings with your spouse, friend or counselor and identify ways to manage these emotions. In doing so, these emotions are less likely to come out in unproductive or hurtful ways toward your child or others in your life. Managing your emotions will enable you to bring the best of yourself into your relationship with your child.

Having grief related to your child's neurodivergence doesn't mean you don't love your child or don't want him. Rather, allowing yourself to feel the feelings that come up will help you get to a place of accepting the child you have and loving him more fully and deeply.

Your child needs you to be the pilot and steady the plane despite the turbulence of being neurodivergent. He needs to know you are in control of yourself and your emotions so that he doesn't feel responsible for you. Managing your emotions helps your child learn to do the same. You are modeling this for him. It also gives your child a sense of security. He can count on you to be a calm, predictable presence in his turbulent world.

It helps to consider where your child may be in his grief process as well. He, too, is grieving the loss that comes with being neurodivergent. Give your child a safe place to express his emotions. This doesn't mean you accept bad behavior. You can set limits around his behavior while at the same time helping him understand the emotions driving his behavior. This can be hard to do while you are struggling with your own emotions.

This is where self-care comes in.

Self-care is critical in getting through the grief process. Having outlets for your grief and breaks from your grief is an important part of taking care of yourself. Self-care involves nurturing yourself and giving yourself grace. Your capacity for managing your life may be impacted by your grief. Be gentle with yourself. As you learn to manage your emotions, you will better manage your life and be better able to support your child in his own grief process.

By managing your emotions, you can provide reassurance to your child that all is well with the world.

GATE FIVE

KNOW YOUR BUTTONS

"Buttons" are events or situations that may bring about feelings of grief (or trauma) related to parenting your neurodivergent child. It is important to recognize your buttons as this will help you learn to better manage your emotions. Knowing your "buttons" can also help you think ahead, problem-solve and develop a plan for how you want to respond when your buttons are pushed (triggered). I've identified some common "buttons" as outlined below, plus possible solutions to managing your grief when triggered.

1) Your Child's Grief

As mentioned previously, your child may be grieving with you. When he comes home hurt and angry because someone made fun of him for being different at school, this can push your "buttons." Your protective instinct may kick in. You may feel sad and angry for him. Your own grief has been triggered. You've been reminded that you don't have a neurotypical child.

It's important to be mindful of your grief and do your best to manage your feelings without reflecting them to your child.

Venting your feelings to your child is not helpful. It can lead to your child feeling anxious and insecure, as now he is focused on your grief vs. his own. This might cause him to feel responsible for your feelings, and for taking care of you. This is called role reversal. This is not a helpful dynamic in your relationship. It is not healthy for your child. It is your job to comfort your child, not the other way around.

Solutions: Normalize and validate your child's feelings. Say "I'm so sorry others are being mean to you. I am sure that hurts your feelings. It's normal to feel hurt when others are not treating you well. What can I do to support you?" Reassure him. Share a story from your childhood of a time when you overcame a struggle. Share stories of others who have demonstrated resilience. Teach your child assertiveness skills for standing up for himself, such as, "It hurts my feelings when you put me down. I would like you to be nicer to me." Encourage your child to seek support from a school counselor or school administrator, or you may need to do so.

2) Past Memories or Trauma

Past trauma or memories can be triggered for you as you raise your special kiddo. Perhaps your child stirs memories of the challenges you faced growing up. Sometimes these memories are stored beside the feelings and beliefs you internalized about yourself at the time. All of this can come flooding back (maybe even unconsciously), adding to your grief process and intensifying your emotions and reactions. When your emotions seem out of proportion to the situation, this can be a clue that perhaps a button is getting pushed, often from your own past.

You might recall how your parents responded to you when you struggled similarly to your own child. Maybe your parents didn't handle your challenges in the best ways, bringing back memories associated with negative feelings and beliefs about yourself. If the apple didn't fall far from the tree and a past memory is triggered, it's important to remember that your child's experience may not be the same as your own. Nor do you have to parent your child in the same way you were parented.

For example, you might recall being bullied in middle school. As your child is entering middle school, you might grow anxious. Your child's developmental age reminds you of being bullied at the same age. If you are not aware of this, you might act in overprotective ways. This can give your child the message that middle school is to be feared.

Similarly, the beliefs you internalized along with past memories or trauma might come to the fore. Be careful to not project your own internal negative labels or beliefs onto your child. Let's say you recall doing poorly in school and were told by your parents that you were lazy. You may have internalized that negative label and indeed believed you were lazy. If you aren't careful, when you see your child struggle similarly you could project this belief onto your child, thinking that he is lazy or even calling him lazy. This will not help his self-esteem nor motivate him. What appears to be "lazy" is more likely a result of his executive function skills deficits. It could also be avoidance due to anxiety.

Solutions: Seek professional help for past experiences or trauma that are still affecting you. Consider EMDR therapy (www.emdr.com) or another trauma-based approach. Be mindful of what is coming up for you and take time to process this so you do not project it onto your child. Remind yourself that your child's experience may not be the same as yours. Think about how you want to handle things differently than your parents did with you. You might make a list of ways you were parented that you don't want to repeat, and identify alternate parenting approaches you prefer to implement.

3) Your Child's Behaviors

Your child may have behaviors that push your buttons. Perhaps he is forgetful. After forgetting his lunch for the third time this week, you are angry at being inconvenienced by having to bring his lunch to school. Maybe he has poor frustration tolerance and struggles to understand his math homework. Homework is often met with meltdowns, which makes you feel frustrated and sad for your child. Maybe he struggles to wake up in the morning and is chronically late to school, causing you to be late to work. You fear losing your job and worry whether he will manage to hold a job one day. You wish he didn't have to struggle so. You wish you had a "normal" child and didn't have to deal with these meltdowns.

Solutions: Be mindful of your emotions. Take time to cool off if needed. Breathe. Do not take your feelings out on your child. Remain calm in talking to your child about his behavior. Educate yourself about his diagnosis. This may help you be more understanding of his behavioral challenges. Know that he is likely having difficulty handling his emotions, which may be driving his behavior. Encourage him to talk about his feelings and needs. Engage your child in problem-solving together (see Gate 7). Remind yourself of your child's strengths and positive qualities. Remind him as well. Recognize frustration as a natural part of the learning process. Encourage persistence. Reassure your child that you will figure this out together.

4) Your Own Thoughts/Beliefs

You might find yourself having negative thoughts or beliefs about your child. These are a symptom of your grief or trauma. Thinking of your child as "bad," "lazy, "stupid" or "broken" can be detrimental to his self-concept, especially if you speak these thoughts out loud. Even if you don't, thinking of your child negatively can evoke your grief and lead you to relate to your child out of frustration, anger or resignation. This can be harmful to your relationship with your child.

Solutions: Seek to understand your child. Educate yourself about his diagnosis. Seek professional guidance to help you understand your child. Work to reframe negative thoughts about your child to more positive ways of thinking about him. Recognize and appreciate your child's strengths and positive qualities. Recognize the progress your child has made.

5) Judgment and Rejection from Others

Your child may experience judgment or rejection from others, triggering his grief as mentioned above. You, too, might experience judgment and rejection as parents of a neurodivergent child. Others might pass judgment on your parenting, assuming your child is acting the way he does because he isn't disciplined properly at home. You might feel guilty or angry in response to feeling blamed or judged. Teachers might make negative assumptions about your child or about you as a parent. You might find friends or family avoiding spending time with you because they don't want to be around your child.

Solutions: Understand that judgment comes from a place of fear and misunderstanding. Don't take it personally. Ask yourself,

"Do I really want to spend time with people who are going to judge me or my child anyway?" Take time to educate others about your child's issues. Provide them with articles or refer them to books about neurodivergence if they are open to learning more. Seek support from others who have neurodivergent children. They are likely to be more understanding.

6) Comparison

You might compare your child to an older or younger sibling and feel he's not measuring up. You might see other children receiving accolades and feel bad that your child is not getting recognition for the cool kid he is. Other parents may talk about the college acceptances their child is receiving. Comparing your child to others can lend itself to grief. Comparison is not helpful. Yet you may do it. It is human nature.

Solutions: Remind yourself that each child is unique. Recognize your child's strengths and positive qualities. Don't compare your child to others but see him as his own gift to this world, that he, too, has something valuable to offer even if it hasn't been discovered yet. Remind yourself that he's not a typical child and likely won't take the typical path in life. But that's OK! It's OK to be different. Remind your child of the same. Tell him, "You do you!"

7) Differences in Parenting Styles

Just as parents of typical children can have different parenting styles, so can parents of neurodivergent children. Differences in parenting styles may heighten conflict between you and your spouse or co-parent due to feelings of underlying grief. As a mom, you can be triggered by your husband's harsh way of handling a situation because you are protective of your neuroatypical child. You might feel your child has enough challenges and doesn't need Dad's harsh approach. Your grief could provoke a more severe reaction on your part to your husband's discipline style. In turn, Dad's harsh approach may reflect his own grief over having a neurodivergent child. Perhaps he expresses his sadness through angry/aggressive parenting.

If you struggle to get on the same page with parenting, beware. This can be harmful to your child. Your child can pick up on these differences and learn to manipulate you or the situation. It can also lead to your child developing an anxious and insecure attachment style.

Solutions: In private (without children around), identify problems that lend themselves to conflict. Discuss an agreeable approach to handling these problems or a solution you can agree on. Present a united front. Do not contradict one another or undermine one another in front of your child. Seek professional help if you struggle to agree on how to approach a problem or have difficulty coming up with solutions.

In Gate Six, we will explore further how to respond rather than react to these challenges.

GATE SIX

RESPOND, DON'T REACT

Viktor Frankl, psychiatrist and Holocaust survivor, wrote this in his trailblazing book, *A Man's Search for Meaning*: "Between stimulus and response there is a space. In that space is our power to choose our response. In our response lies our growth and freedom."

There is a difference between reacting and responding. When your "buttons" get pushed and you allow your emotions to dictate your actions, you are reacting. On the other hand, learning to pause gives you space that allows you the freedom to choose how you want to react. This is responding.

You alone are responsible for the choices you make when your "buttons" are pushed. You can say or do things that may make it worse for yourself and your relationship with your child. Or you can make choices that will honor your feelings and help you move through them in a positive way while also keeping your relationship intact.

Pause...

When you notice your "buttons" have been pushed, pause. As previously mentioned, this pause gives you time to think about what triggered you and how you want to respond. The pause can be a brief moment or longer if needed. There is nothing wrong with saying to your child, "I'm angry right now and I need some time to cool off. Let's discuss this later." Saying this models for your child a coping skill he can use when triggered. This will be beneficial to him in managing his own emotions.

Breathe...

Taking a deep breath or two or three or more during the pause gives you time to calm down. Deep breathing has a calming effect on your nervous system, helps lower your blood pressure and heart rate and helps your mind and body to relax. You are more likely to make better choices in any given situation when you can come from a calm place vs. a place of heightened emotions. Using your breathing is an effective tool to calm yourself down. While doing so you are buying time to think about how you want to respond.

Name The Feeling...

When your "buttons" are pushed, it helps to identify the emotion that is triggered and verbally name it. The act of naming your emotion engages the left side of your brain, where your language centers are located (also the logical and rational side of your brain). It also brings balance to the right side of the brain, where emotions are experienced. When your left and right brain work together, you are more likely to respond in a more balanced way.

Regulate Emotions...

The pause allows you to identify what pushed your buttons and gives you time to problem-solve the situation. First, though, you might need to problem-solve around your feelings. If angered, you might think about what choices you can make to calm yourself down. When emotions are high, your ability to problem-solve is impeded. This is a result of brain function and is backed up by science. Conversations typically don't go well when in a heightened emotional state. Once calm, though, you can have a conversation about what pushed your "buttons" in the first place and engage your problem-solving skills.

Ways to regulate your emotions include...

- Taking slow, deep breaths
- Focusing on relaxing your body
- Moving your body (exercise)
- Moving to another room or location
- Spending time alone
- Journaling
- Spending time in nature
- Snuggling with your pet
- Wrapping yourself in a blanket (weighted blankets rock)
- Engaging in a creative outlet (drawing, painting, coloring, playing an instrument, writing poetry)
- Thinking of a positive memory or looking at photos
- Making a gratitude list or thinking of the positives in a situation
- Getting a massage
- Practicing mindfulness (use a mindfulness app)

- Taking a hot bath or shower
- Taking a nap
- Talking to a friend, loved one or professional

I have had kid clients arrive red-faced and fuming following a blow-up in the car on the way to my office. When this happens, I pull out my sandbox and suggest they dig their hands into the sand. It is amazing how effective this is, and how their anger quickly sifts away just as kinetic sand shifts its shape. Likewise, when I have met with kids via telehealth I have witnessed the palpable power of their pets. One minute the teen I'm working with is in a tirade about how terrible his parents are. Then his cat climbs in his lap and I watch his anger melt away.

Having ways to self-soothe and calm yourself is critical in your role as a parent. It's also important to help your child find ways he can learn to regulate his emotions.

SOLVING PROBLEMS

Here are steps that can be helpful in problem-solving:

Identify The Problem

Problem-solving first involves identifying the problem. It's hard to solve a problem if you don't know what it is. It's important to be on the same page, as it is possible you think the problem is one thing and your child, spouse or teacher thinks it's something else. You will spin your wheels and get nowhere if you try to problem-solve different problems instead of the same one.

Brainstorm Solutions

The next step in problem-solving is to brainstorm solutions. I suggest doing this together with your child. Sometimes children aren't given enough credit for being able to solve problems. You might think you know best or think your life experience gives you an advantage when it comes to problem-solving. But in my experience, I am almost always amazed by what children come up with and how creative they can be with their solutions. Creative problem-solving is a strength of neurodivergent children. Be sure to recognize this as a strength of theirs and encourage it. Engaging them in this process of solving their own problems builds their confidence and empowers them to one day solve their problems independently. It also gets them to buy into the solution.

Evaluate Possible Solutions

Once solutions have been brainstormed, it's time to decide on one. This may involve thinking of the pros/cons of each solution to determine which seems to be the best one.

Pick The Solution You Think Is Likely To Work Best

Once a solution is determined, it's time to implement it. It's important to stick with a solution for a period of time as sometimes it may not solve a problem immediately. But given time, it may. The opposite can also be true. Sometimes a solution works in the short-term but then over time stops working. That's when another solution needs to be tried.

Evaluate If The Solution Solved The Problem

After a period of time, evaluating whether the solution solved the problem is important. If you don't take this step and you keep implementing a solution that's not working, frustration will ensue.

If Not, Try Another Solution

It may be that another solution needs to be tried until the problem is resolved.

Repeat This Process Until The Problem Is Resolved

For more information about collaborative problem-solving, I recommend reading Dr. Ross Greene's book, *The Explosive Child.* Check out his "Collaborative and Proactive Solutions." You can find the trauma-informed, neurodiversity-affirming model at www.livesinthebalance.org. He also offers workshops, which are well worth the expense!

It is important to know that your child's behaviors are likely not intentional. However, if you react to his behaviors, they may become intentional because he has now learned he has power over you by getting a rise out of you. What kid doesn't want power, especially when they are feeling powerless???

The majority of the time when a child is displaying an undesirable behavior it is out of his own grief or other feelings with which he is struggling. Or it could be related to lagging skills due to his executive function deficits.

I gave the example previously of a child repeatedly forgetting his lunch. If this was your son, rather than solving the problem for him, it's the perfect opportunity to help him learn problem-solving skills.

Find a time to sit down with him and talk calmly about the

problem. First, identify the problem and the negative impact it's having. You might say something like, "I've noticed you've been forgetting your lunch quite often, three days this week in fact. The problem with this is that I'm having to take time out of my day to bring it to you. This is causing frustration for me. Is this a problem for you, too? How so?"

Then encourage your child to brainstorm solutions: "Do you have any ideas that might help you remember your lunch each day?" If he can't come up with solutions, you might suggest some: "Perhaps we could write a reminder on a Post-It note and put it on the front door. Or you could buy your lunch when you forget to bring it. Which solution do you prefer?"

Together you can decide a course of action. It helps to monitor how the solution is working and check back in with one another about whether the solution solved the problem. If so, great! If not, try another solution.

Another example is the child who struggles with his math homework, gets easily frustrated and has meltdowns. Perhaps after brainstorming together, he comes up with the solution to go outside and jump on the trampoline with you for 10 minutes the next time he gets frustrated. This might help relieve stress, improve moods (his and yours) and allow his brain to regulate before getting back to homework.

If he continues to have math meltdowns on a regular basis despite the outdoor break, try another solution. He could stay after school or go in early for extra help from his teacher. Perhaps it's time to hire a math tutor. Your child will likely save his worst behavior for you but be on his best behavior for others. Hiring a tutor might eliminate his meltdowns and eradicate stress and conflict in your relationship.

Reframe

When the trigger is your own negative thoughts and beliefs about your child, rather than thinking of your child as "bad," "lazy" or "unmotivated," learn to reframe your thoughts. This is where understanding your child's diagnosis and how it impacts his learning and behavior is crucial. If you understand that ADHD leads to your child being impulsive, you are less likely to think of his behavior as "bad." Instead of thinking of him as lazy, you can recognize that he has trouble getting started on things and struggles with organization and planning skills (taking initiative). Or you can identify that he is anxious and thus avoiding. These more positive explanations can help you better help your child. When you think your child is lazy or unmotivated, you might feel frustrated and angry and give up trying to help him or react in ways that may hurt your relationship with him. But when you recognize that his struggles are not personal to him (or you) but related to his emotions or brain function, you are more likely to feel positively and want to help him. Likewise, you can help your child reframe negative thoughts and beliefs he has about himself to more positive ones.

Plan Ahead

When you know your "buttons" (or your child's) you can plan ahead for them. For instance, if your child gets easily overstimulated in crowded and loud places and acts up when this happens, together you can identify what might help him in these situations and plan accordingly. The solution might be for him to wear noise-canceling headphones the next time you go to a baseball game. Or if your husband's harsh tone with your child pushes your buttons, perhaps you discuss it with your husband and agree on a signal to alert him to his tone.

If your buttons get pushed by others asking you what college your child is going to (as he's not going to college), you can have a prepared response for these sorts of questions. Maybe you say something like, "He's taking a gap year to figure out what he wants to do."

Let Go

Sometimes your "buttons" get pushed because of your own expectations and unwillingness to change or let go of these expectations. With neurodivergent children you may need to modify or let go of unrealistic expectations. Your child may not be able to do what the typical child can do due to differences in how his brain is wired.

If you are telling your child to do multiple things at a time, for example "Brush your teeth, get your shoes on, put your homework in your backpack and get your lunch. I'll meet you in the car," and he is forgetting some steps or not following directions to your satisfaction, it is you who needs to change, not him. You may need to give him one or two things to do at a time, not three or four.

In school, a typical child may be able to get 20 math problems done in 20 minutes. A neurodivergent child with a math disability may take twice as long on the same number of math problems. Some teachers don't seem to understand this, or care, and aren't willing to reduce work for these kids. They hold them to the same standards as typical children. I've seen this even when a child has an IEP or 504 plan. This can result in hours of homework that overwhelm and exhaust the neurodivergent child. After a while, the neurodivergent child may begin to not care about doing homework and doing well in school. He begins to give up (learned helplessness). It would be so much easier if teachers would be willing to let go of and/ or adjust their expectations. If typical kids are spending 20 minutes on math each night and completing 20 problems, have the neurodivergent child do 10 problems in the same amount of time. It's not difficult to let go of or change expectations.

Sometimes teachers worry that it won't be fair to other students. What's not fair is holding neurodivergent kids to the same standards as neurotypical kids. If your child's teacher hesitates to make accommodations for this reason, advocate that "Fair is not equal." In other words, because we are all different we sometimes have different needs. Accommodations sometimes need to be made to level the playing field.

Don't be prideful. Don't think adults know best. Believe it or not, your child knows a lot more than you might give him credit for. Ask for your child's input about what he needs and what would be helpful to him. He will often know or can figure it out! He is capable of problem-solving with you. Have faith in him!

Encourage Independence

It's natural to "overdo" and "overparent" your neurodivergent child. However, doing so can impede his independence and lead to dependency on you. You could easily become the helicopter parent out of your own grief response to your child's struggles. It's important to recognize if this is happening or your child may not grow into the responsible, independent child you are meant to raise. That is your task as a parent.

Ask yourself, "Am I doing things for my child that he can do for himself?" If so, identify what those things are and let go! Don't do it all at once. Gradually hold your child more responsible for taking on these tasks—one at a time. This is called a scaffolding approach. Encouraging your child's independence will help him grow into a more confident adult.

It is important for your child to take on more responsibility for himself with the goal of becoming independent by adulthood. However, adulthood doesn't necessarily mean that the moment your child turns 18 he will be capable of being completely independent. Every child has his own timeline. One child may be ready to launch at 18, another not until he is 24.

A conundrum can happen with neurodivergent children. It is usually in middle school and into high school when children experience a normal developmental drive to be more independent and lean less on parents for help. Neurodivergent kids experience this natural drive yet tend to lack the skills to be as independent as their neurotypical peers. In other words, they need help from their parents or other adults longer than the typical child. This can lend to inner conflict for them and greater conflict in the parent-child relationship. Lean on other adults to offer support to your child—tutors, therapists, aunts, uncles, grandparents, neighbors, friends. At this stage in the game, your child will be more open to guidance from others.

"It takes a village!" to raise these neurospicy kids.

Neuroatypical children (any child, really) may need to understand and be told that asking for and accepting help will allow them to grow into becoming more independent. It may help to tell your child that even adults need help sometimes. We are always learning and growing. It's impossible to know everything. Asking for help and being open to receiving it allows us to continue to grow and learn throughout life.

Recognize What Is In Our Control (And What Isn't)

As badly as you may wish for your child to be a typical child or for parenting him to be easier, it's important to recognize that this is not within your control. These kids are difficult, challenging and exhausting to parent at times. This is not something you can change. The sooner you accept this reality, the easier it will be to get in the groove of parenting your child and be open to strategies that will make life with him easier.

When swimming in a river, it is much easier to go with the flow of the water rather than against it. Refusing to accept that your child is neurodivergent and that you have to approach the challenge of raising him differently is like swimming against the current. You cannot change who your child is and how he is wired. It's better to accept him for who he is and work with what you've been given. Remember, you can't control your child. But you can control how you react to him and his behaviors.

GATE SEVEN

MANAGING BURNOUT
AND THE IMPORTANCE OF SELF-CARE

According to the World Health Organization, burnout is an occupational condition resulting from chronic workplace stress that has not been successfully managed. Just as we can experience burnout in a job or career, parenting can lead to burnout. After all, it is our most important job, one in which we invest our heart and soul.

I have seen many parents of neurodivergent children reach the point of sheer exhaustion. Parental burnout is defined by a study published in "Clinical Psychological Science" (2019) as "overwhelming exhaustion related to one's parental role, an emotional distancing from one's children and a sense of parental ineffectiveness."

According to Noam Shpancer, Ph.D., stress and exhaustion can escalate to the level of burnout for 20 percent of parents and even higher for parents of children with chronic illness.[*]

---

[*] Noam Shpancer, Ph.D. "Parental Burnout: When Parenting Becomes Too Much," *Psychology Today*, August 1, 2023.

I imagine the rates of burnout are also higher for parents raising neurodivergent children. Having a neurodivergent child adds more time and energy to the parental load. In addition to the typical parenting tasks, you likely juggle more frequent communication with teachers and having to advocate for your child's needs in school; multiple appointments with professionals throughout the week; extended time spent on homework; getting prescriptions filled and managing medications; managing your child's executive function deficits, and dealing with your child's more challenging behaviors.

"10 Ways to Overcome Parental Burnout" (February 28, 2021) on autismadhdconnection.com references a study from the University of Wisconsin-Madison which found that mothers of autistic children spent two hours more per day caring for their children than mothers of neurotypical children. These moms were reported to be more than two times as likely to become tired on a given day and three times more likely to experience a stressful event. This study found that mothers of children with autism have similar stress levels as combat soldiers.

Additionally, your risk for burnout is likely amplified if you are a neurodivergent parent, in other words if you have LD, ADHD or Autism yourself. In an ADDitude magazine article dated March 4, 2024 — "Rising From ADHD Burnout: A Recovery Kit for Women" — chronic stress is identified as a common problem for women with ADHD. Executive dysfunction, which goes along with ADHD, is identified as leading to more cognitive energy expended to get through daily activities. Additionally, emotional dysregulation can lead to more intense feelings that can consume thoughts and drain energy. This can lead to rumination, stress and feeling overwhelmed. Women with ADHD may also find that hormonal changes throughout their menstrual cycle can impact energy levels as well as their ADHD symptoms.

As you can imagine, having neurodivergence yourself would only add to the stress of parenting these challenging kids.

Additional stressors may put you over the edge even faster:

- Multiple children with neurodivergence
- Job stress
- Financial stress
- Health/mental health issues
- Marital discord
- Divorce/coparenting
- Caring for aging parents
- Grief/loss
- Trauma

It is important to recognize the stress you are under and signs of burnout so you can take the necessary steps to recover from it.

Signs Of Burnout

- Exhaustion/lack of energy
- Cynicism or negative outlook
- Feeling ineffective/reduced productivity or performance
- Lack of enjoyment
- Detachment from others
- Irritability or anger
- Less patient/more yelling

- Difficulty concentrating
- Difficulty sleeping
- Body aches/pains
- High blood pressure
- Significant weight gain/loss
- Use of alcohol or drugs to cope
- Anxiety/depression

Now that you know the signs to look for, here are 10 tips to prevent burnout:

- Educate yourself on your child's diagnosis.
- Get organized.
- Delegate tasks.
- Ask for or hire help.
- Engage problem-solving skills.
- Pick your battles.
- Lower expectations of yourself and others.
- Set boundaries as needed.
- Connect with other parents of neurodivergent kids.
- Schedule breaks.

Additionally, engaging in regular self-care is important to prevent and recover from burnout. Recovery can involve more radical self-care. What I mean by this is a more intensive focus on and practice of self-care.

So let's talk self-care.

I've already shared the analogy of putting on your oxygen mask to take care of yourself before you take care of your child.

Another analogy to consider…

When do you fill up the gas tank on your car? Do you wait until the empty light comes on? I know I used to. In fact, when it came on, I still didn't rush to fill up. I knew I had 20 or so miles before I'd run out of gas. I pushed it to the limit. I dare say my self-care was dangerously similar.

You can think about self-care like filling up your gas tank. You need to learn to pay attention to the signals that you are running out of gas and not wait until you are on empty to fill up. I recommend practicing this concept by filling up your car when it's at a half-tank rather than waiting until the empty light comes on. Once you master this (with your car), work on applying this to your own self-care. Identify signals that you are getting depleted. Maybe you notice you are less patient, more snappy and can't wait to get in bed. When you notice these signals, it's time to fill up with self-care.

Out of love and concern it is natural to feel protective of your neurodivergent child. When you have a child who is struggling, your "mama bear" goes into overdrive. It is all too easy to pour yourself into caring for your child to the point of neglecting yourself. I know I did.

I didn't expect parenting to be as challenging as it turned out to be. None of us do. At some point, reality set in that this was the hand I'd been dealt, that it wasn't going to change or get easier. Coming to that place of acceptance was a critical step for me.

I began to let go of what I couldn't control and started to focus on myself and what was within my control. I sought professional help, which helped me recognize the importance of self-care. I began to reclaim time for myself. I thought about the times when I felt happy and realized I needed to create more of those moments in my life. I worked on developing my social support. I got together with old friends and made new ones. I joined a weekly prayer group and women's wellness group. I re-engaged in activities I enjoyed in the past, like hiking, yoga, writing poetry and going to concerts and musicals. I discovered new interests like riding motorcycles and playing pickleball. I started getting massages and pedicures on occasion. I bought myself nicer clothes than the second-hand ones I was accustomed to getting for myself. I went to a yoga retreat center one weekend and even went to a hotel on occasion to get a much-needed break and time for myself.

I started making myself, my needs and my happiness a priority. Of course, it became easier to do so as my children entered the teen and young adult years.

My motto became, "If I don't take care of myself, no one else will." As I did, my life began to change. Circumstances didn't change necessarily. But my mindset did and with it my approach as a parent. With improved self-care, I found that I had more energy to handle the challenges that continued to come my way.

I know that when I first started practicing self-care, it felt a little selfish. I wasn't used to focusing on myself, putting myself first. I felt guilty for taking time away from my family. I had buyer's remorse after treating myself to a nice piece of clothing. I had trouble relaxing during a massage, thinking of the cost. But I kept practicing. Just like anything else, we don't get good at it by doing it once or twice. Over time, as I kept practicing self-care, it became more natural. I realized how critical it was to my own mental health and well-being.

I also began to recognize that it was helping me to show up differently as a parent. I was happier, more patient and calmer in handling parenting challenges. I began to recognize that not only did I deserve self-care, it was critical to my survival as a parent and in having a positive relationship with my children. I even became protective of time for myself. Sometimes I wouldn't even let my loved ones know when I was having "me" time. I let it be my little secret, which made it special and more fun. It was a gift I learned to give myself.

It may help to make a list of self-care practices that you enjoy. I recommend posting these practices where you can remind yourself to do them. I also recommend scheduling your self-care. It is helpful to actually make an appointment with yourself and add it to your calendar whether it's time you plan to go to a yoga class or have lunch with a friend. You are more likely to stick to it when you have a plan in place.

It doesn't stop there. You might find that when you schedule something for yourself, something else comes up and you are quick to cave. Don't! Learn to hold your boundaries and not give into other distractions or people who demand your time.

This is about learning to put yourself first and prioritize YOU!!!

This means you will need to get good at saying "No!" to others and to have the courage to be disliked. Others may not be pleased at first. That's OK! It is not your job to please the world! In fact, if you continue to put others before yourself, you are training them to put you last. By valuing yourself, you are teaching others in your life to value you as well.

When I asked parents I interviewed about burnout, one dad identified that he swallowed his feelings and acknowledged that he was irritable, edgy and hateful (at times). Another dad identified being in fight-or-flight mode and admitted "It's survival day to day." A few moms acknowledged that they didn't manage their feelings well. Several identified being exhausted emotionally. Another mom claimed to not have enough time to manage her feelings. She said, "By the time I've done everything I need to do to manage her, it's bedtime."

When asked about self-care, one mom said, "A primal scream does the soul well." A dad mentioned "Waving the white flag."

Other parents identified self-care practices, including...

- Going to therapy
- Taking medication
- Connecting with other parents of neurodivergent kids
- Finding a support group
- Talking to friends
- Recognizing successes
- Having personal goals and accomplishments
- Taking up a hobby
- Having a good cry
- Going for a drive
- Appreciating magic moments (gratitude)
- Taking breaks
- Having radical fun

One mom ran a 100-mile race. She'd never been to therapy. Running was her therapy. Another mom wisely stated, "I learned to let go. I knew she was going to struggle but it's her struggle."

Another mom gave up her full-time leadership position at work and went part-time. I look back and wish I had given up my full-time job and leaped into private practice sooner. I would have been able to work fewer hours and have more flexibility with my schedule and time. This would have alleviated much of my stress. You may need to consider a job or career change to reduce stress.

Additional self-care practices for mind, body and spirit:

Mind

- Use a planner or to-do list.
- Have a checklist for your morning and evening routines.
- Use a medication box to keep track of medications.
- Practice mindfulness or meditation.
- Reframe negative thoughts to positive ones.
- Use positive self-talk. For example, "I've got this!"
- Use a mantra. For example, "This, too, shall pass."
- Journal.
- Visualize a place you feel safe, calm and relaxed.
- Get organized.
- Take a mental health day (or two or three) off from work.

Body

- Eat three healthy meals per day.
- Limit or eliminate alcohol and other drugs.
- Exercise. For example, walk, run, hike, take a fitness class, play a sport, do yoga.
- Use diaphragmatic breathing. Also known as "belly breathing," this involves taking long, slow, deep breaths.
- Get a massage.
- Get a manicure, pedicure or facial.

- Practice progressive muscle relaxation. This involves tensing and releasing muscle groups, starting at the feet and progressing to the top of your body.
- Find time to rest and relax. Take a nap.
- Treat yourself to your favorite comfort food.
- Call in sick to work.

Spirit

- Engage in a creative activity. Write poetry or a personal essay, draw, paint, color, craft, build something.
- Engage in a favorite hobby.
- Spend time in nature.
- Practice gratitude.
- Listen to music/play an instrument.
- Laugh. Watch a comedy on TV, go to a comedy show, spend time with a funny friend.
- Do something adventurous. How about ziplining, whitewater rafting, skydiving, bungee-jumping or riding on a motorcycle.
- Plan a weekend away.
- Take a vacation.
- Go on a retreat.
- Get together with a friend.
- Go to a therapist.
- Go to church. Pray.
- Volunteer to serve others.

How much self-care you need may depend on how burned out you are. For example, if you are a working parent with one or two symptoms of burnout, taking a day or two off from work and focusing that time on self-care may be enough to fill your tank back up. Others may suffer from more severe burnout and need to take a week or more off from work. I have had clients whom I recommended go on short-term disability. You will have to look into what your benefits include and whether this is the best choice for you. Additionally, under the Family and Medical Leave Act (FMLA), employees can take up to 12 weeks of unpaid leave to care for a serious health condition. This is typically for when burnout has led to more serious psychological problems like anxiety, depression or trauma. In these cases, it is imperative that a mental health professional be involved in your care.

GATE EIGHT

SEEK SUPPORT AND KNOW YOUR RESOURCES

Knowing you can count on support is crucial to managing the stresses of life, whatever they are.

In my interviews with parents of neurodivergent children, many spoke of a lack of such support from friends and family—the very people they hoped they could turn to. Many parents expressed feeling alone, isolated and misunderstood at times, and felt their parenting called into question. They felt as if they were being blamed for their child's misbehavior. They felt their child being judged by those closest to him. They recognized that their child faced rejection by peers and other parents.

When friends and family don't understand your child and the challenges you face as a parent, you can help by educating them about your child's diagnosis and how this lends itself to his behavioral challenges. You can refer them to books, articles and websites you have found informative and helpful.

In that same spirit, when spending time with friends or family or leaving your child in their care, provide strategies that have helped you in managing your child's behavior and meeting his needs. This is equally important when leaving your child in the care of a babysitter or respite care worker.

This lack of support is a reality for many parents of neurodivergent children. But rather than discouraging you, let it inspire you to seek what you and your child need. If you can't find it, help make it happen!

Connect with parents of other neurodivergent kids.

Ask your child's school counselor to consider starting a support group for parents. Share your name and contact information with other parents who have children with neurodivergence.

Search for support groups in your area or consider starting one on your own. You might search for an online support group or Facebook group.

Having a place to share the stresses and challenges of parenting your neurodivergent child can help you feel less alone. Having other parents who "get it" can help more than you can imagine. It also gives you a place to learn and share resources with other parents who face similar challenges.

Of the parents I interviewed, those who found support seemed to fare better. They seemed to have a more positive outlook and attitude as they parented their children. They seemed to suffer less burnout.

Here are organizations where you can learn more about Learning Disabilities, Attention Deficit Hyperactivity Disorder (ADHD), Autism and other challenges, and also find support:

- **Children and Adults with Attention Deficit/ Hyperactivity Disorder (CHADD)**. www.chadd.org.
- **Inattentive ADHD Coalition.** www.iadhd.org.
- **ADDA (Attention Deficit Disorder Association)**. www.add.org.
- **Understood.** www.understood.org.
- **Child Mind Institute**. www.childmind.org.
- **Autism and ADHD Connection.** www. autismadhdconnection.com.
- **Autism Society.** www.autismsociety.org.
- **Learning Disabilities Association of America.** www. ldaamerica.org.
- **International Dyslexia Association.** www.dyslexiaida. org.
- **National Institute of Mental Health (NIMH).** www. nimh.nih.gov.
- **National Alliance on Mental Illness.** www.nami.org.

Many of these national organizations have state or local chapters. Search in your area to find what's available to you.

Additionally, there are some valuable podcasts addressing neurodivergence. Check these out:
- "Attitude: Strategies and Support for ADHD and LD."
- "Divergent Conversations: A Neurodivergent Podcast."
- "How To ADHD."
- "Uniquely Human."
- "ADHD is Awesome."

Here are some of my favorite books and ones recommended by my colleagues:

- *Taking Charge of ADHD* by Russell A. Barkley, Ph.D.
- *Driven to Distraction* by Edward M. Hallowell, M.D. & John Ratey, M.D.
- *ADHD Is Awesome: A Guide to (Mostly Thriving) with ADHD* by Penn and Kim Holderness.
- *Understanding Girls with ADHD* by Kathleen G. Nadeau, Ph.D., Ellen B. Littman, Ph.D. and Patricia O. Quinn, M.D.
- *The Explosive Child: A New Approach for Understanding and Parenting Easily Frustrated, Chronically Inflexible Children* by Ross W. Greene, Ph.D.
- *A Parent's Guide to High-Functioning Autism Spectrum Disorder: How to Meet the Challenges and Help Your Child Thrive* by Sally Ozonoff, Ph.D., Geraldine Dawson, Ph.D. and James C. McPartland, Ph.D.
- *Autism in Heels* by Jennifer Cooke O'Toole.
- *Dyslexia: A Complete Guide for Parents and Those Who Help Them* by Gavin Reid.
- *The Dyslexia Empowerment Plan* by Ben Foss.
- *Nonverbal Learning Disabilities at School* by Pamela B. Tanguay.
- *It's So Much Work To Be Your Friend: Helping The Child With Learning Disabilities Find Social Success* by Richard Lavoie and Michelle Ruiner.
- *Dysgraphia: A Parent's Guide to Understanding Dysgraphia and Helping a Dysgraphic Child* by Nathan G. Brant.

Additionally, there are books written for children to help them better understand differences, learning disabilities, ADHD and Autism Spectrum Disorder:

- *Red: A Crayon's Story* by Michael Hall.
- *Spoon* by Amy Krouse Rosenthal and Scott Magoon.
- *Thank you, Mr. Falker* by Patricia Polacco.
- *Fish in a Tree* by Lynda Mullaly Hunt.
- *It's Called Dyslexia* by Jennifer Moore-Mallinos.
- *The Survival Guide For Kids with LD* by Garry Fisher, Ph.D. and Rhoda Cummings, Ed.D.
- *All dogs have ADHD* by Kathy Hoopman.
- *The Survival Guide for Kids with ADHD* by John F. Taylor, Ph.D.
- *Learning to Slow Down & Pay Attention* by Kathleen G. Nadeau, Ph.D. and Ellen B. Dixon, Ph.D.
- *The Survival Guide for Kids with Autism Spectrum Disorder* by Elizabeth Verdick and Elizabeth Reeve, M.D.
- *The Asperkid's Secret Book of Social Rules* by Jennifer Cook O'Toole.

There are many, many other books on neurodivergence. These are just ones I or my colleagues have read that come recommended.

As far as parenting information and guidance, I highly recommend Ross Greene's "Collaborate and Proactive Solutions" model for parenting neurodivergent children. Go to his website at **www.livesinthebalance.org** to learn more. He offers workshops for parents, educators and other professionals. His book, *The Explosive Child: A New Approach for Understanding and Parenting Easily Frustrated, Chronically Inflexible Children* is a must read.

I also highly recommend Dan Siegel's book, *No Drama Discipline: The Whole Brain Way to Calm the Chaos and Nurture Your Child's Developing Mind.*

Additionally, *ADDitude Magazine* is my favorite resource for all things ADHD and LD. You can sign up to receive their magazine. They offer free webinars as well. Visit **www. additudemag.com.**

Neurodivergent children often struggle with social skills. Check out Michelle Garcia Winner's work at **www. socialthinking.com.** She has a lot of resources and also offers workshops on helping your child develop self-regulation and social skills.

When To Seek Professional Help

If you recognize that you are experiencing burnout, it may be time to seek the help of a mental health professional.

Seek professional guidance if you are struggling to manage your child's behaviors without yelling or frequent consequences/punishment.

If you and your spouse are struggling to get on the same page with parenting, it is advisable to seek marital counseling.

Ongoing conflict with an ex-spouse around co-parenting issues may also call for finding a mental health therapist who specializes in working with divorced families and co-parenting issues.

If you believe you or your spouse could also be neurodivergent and have not yet been diagnosed you may want to seek a neuropsychological evaluation from a neuropsychologist.

If you are neurodivergent there is a strong chance you may have an anxiety disorder, depression, bipolar disorder or other co-morbid psychiatric disorder. According to the ADAA (Anxiety and Depression Association of America), fifty percent of adults with ADHD also suffer from an anxiety disorder. It is advisable to seek counseling if you need help managing any mental health disorder.

If past trauma is coming up as a result of parenting your neurodivergent child, conflict in your home or having had traumatic experiences with your neurodivergent child (such as self-harm, a suicide attempt, drug-related issues) you may benefit from professional support and treatment. There are trauma-specific approaches such as Eye Movement Desensitization Reprocessing (EMDR), Brainspotting, Accelerated Resolution Therapy, and The Rewind Technique that can help reduce symptoms of trauma. Be sure the professional you seek out is trained in one of these approaches.

See a psychiatrist if you are considering going on medication to manage a mental health disorder. Your primary care physician can also prescribe, but a psychiatrist specializes in working with psychiatric conditions and medications. Nurse practitioners and physician assistants can also prescribe.

In all cases, be sure to find a professional who has training and expertise in neurodivergence.

If you are experiencing a mental health emergency or your child is in crisis, call or text the suicide hotline at 9-8-8 or text TALK to 741741. In an emergency, call 911.

Seeking help is never something to be ashamed of. Everyone needs help sometimes. Talking to a professional can alleviate stress by helping to get things off your mind. It can help to have an objective person give feedback and make suggestions, someone who isn't involved in your situation. Mental health therapists can provide strategies for managing executive function deficits and teach skills for managing symptoms of anxiety and depression. You can reach out to your primary care physician for a referral or contact your insurance company to find a therapist covered by your insurance plan. You might ask family members or friends for a referral.

Another great resource for finding a therapist in your area is **www.psychologytoday.com.** Each therapist has a profile so you can read about them and learn about their specialty areas and approach. Many therapists offer a free initial consult.

Finding the right therapist, one who is a good fit for you and your family, is vital. I tell my clients this right off the bat. I let them know they need to feel comfortable with me or they won't fully benefit. I let them know I take no offense if they decide it's not a good fit. Many therapists offer a free initial consult, though it may only be 15 minutes or so. Take advantage of this. It will help you to know if you connect with the person or not.

Mental health clinicians typically have a Master's degree in counseling or social work or may have a Ph.D. or Psy.D. after their name. The title of the license to practice may be different in each state.

Go to NAMI's website — www.nami.org/About-Mental-Illness/Treatments/Types-of-Mental-Health-Professionals — to learn more about different types of mental health professionals to help you determine which type of professional can best meet your needs.

Don't be afraid to ask the therapist you are meeting with about his or her credentials, years of experience, training, specialties and the like.

The important thing to take away from this chapter — from this entire book — is that **you are not alone**. Support and help are available. You just have to be proactive and reach out.

POSTSCRIPT

YOUR FINAL DESTINATION: MEANING–MAKING

This challenging yet wonderful journey you are on as a parent of a neurodivergent child may not be over. As it is often said, "A parent's job is never done." Yet, as you navigate the grief process and manage the turbulence by practicing self-care, I hope you experience joy in parenting your neurodivergent child. I hope you recognize all the ways in which he is a unique and special human being. I hope you cherish the gift you've been given in parenting him. I hope you begin to make meaning from your experience.

A butterfly's struggle to push through its cocoon is the very thing it needs to strengthen its wings so it can fly. In that spirit, perhaps you can recognize the ways in which the challenges of parenting your child has helped you grow stronger as a person and as a parent. Perhaps you've learned patience or perseverance, which will serve you well as you continue on this journey. Maybe you've learned how to better manage your feelings or to love more deeply. Maybe you've learned to fight for your child's rights and this has helped you stand up for yourself. Maybe you've become a badass! Have you gained a deeper understanding of the world? Is it possible you have developed more compassion for all humans who struggle in some way?

You do, of course, understand that there is cruelty in the world, that not all humans are kind to those who are different.

Yet your experience has taught you to hold your head high. In turn, you have taught your child to do the same. You've taught him to rise above adversity, and that his life has value.

Sometimes when we go through difficult times, it is hard to see past the dark cloud that casts its shadow on our soul. It is important to have hope and know that the sun will shine again. Glimmers of light can shine through even the darkest of clouds. I encourage you to look for the glimmers.

Be intentional in looking for the lessons life has to teach you. Making meaning from your grief can propel you to acceptance and beyond. You can use your learning and knowledge for good. You can use it to propel change in systems and laws by continuing to advocate for children with neurodivergence. You can raise money to support your favorite organization or cause in support of neurodivergence. You can raise awareness by sharing information on social media. You can take your experience and offer understanding, compassion and support to other parents who may be starting on this journey or who are already struggling. You can offer a parenting break by watching a friend's neurodivergent child. You can write a book. Sometimes just a hand on the shoulder, a soft look into someone's suffering soul and an "I get it" can go a long way.

I challenge you to make meaning from your parenting journey. Find some way to pay it forward. Be a glimmer of light for someone else. Pass it on. There can be joy on this journey. It is my hope that this book helps you get to that final destination...joy.

About the Author

Diane Reid Lyon, MA, LCMHC, NCC is a Licensed Clinical Mental Health Counselor in private practice in Matthews, N.C. Diane specializes in working with neurodivergent children/teens and adults with Attention Deficit Hyperactivity Disorder. She is also neurodivergent herself (ADHD). She has a blended family, or as she calls it, the mini-Brady Bunch. In her free time, Diane enjoys hiking, yoga, playing pickleball and writing poetry. Her heart is happiest when spending time with her family, friends and two dogs.

Dear Reader

Thank you. I hope you found counsel and inspiration for your journey.

If so, I invite you to share a positive review or comment online. Reach out to relevant websites, platforms and support groups. Post a blog or a blurb on Twitter, Facebook and the like. Recommend it to parents and other caregivers who are raising a neurodivergent child. Give a heads up to your child's teachers, school administrators, counselors and physicians.

I'd embrace the chance to speak to book clubs, parent gatherings, and school, civic, business, and faith groups. We can talk in person or via Zoom. Reach me at:

www.caringforyourselfbook.com

A central theme of my book is that we do not face these challenges alone. Together, we can care for our children by taking care of ourselves.

With Deep Appreciation,
Diane Reid Lyon

Caring for Yourself, Caring for Your Neurodivergent Child is available for purchase at www.caringforyourselfbook.com. In Charlotte, N.C., you can purchase it at Park Road Books in Park Road Shopping Center. Cost is $20 plus tax, shipping and handling.

Printed in Great Britain
by Amazon

46504420R00066